WHEN THE

Father

HOLDS YOU

Close

A JOURNEY TO DEEPER INTIMACY WITH GOD

CYNTHIA HEALD

THOMAS NELSON PUBLISHERS
Nashville

Published in Nashville, Tennessee, by Thomas Nelson, Inc.

Published in association with the literary agency of Alive Communications, 1465 Kelly Johnson Blvd., Suite 320, Colorado Springs, CO 80920.

Library of Congress Cataloging–in–Publication Data

Heald, Cynthia.
    When the father holds you close: a journey to deeper intimacy with God / Cynthia Heald.
        p. cm.
    ISBN 0-7852-7241-0
    1. Spiritual life—Christianity.   2. Intimacy (Psychology)—Religious aspects—Christianity. I. Title.
    BV4501.2.H36885 1999
    231.7—dc21

                                                                99–15857
                                                                CIP

Printed in the United States of America.
1 2 3 4 5 6 BVG 04 03 02 01 00 99

Contents

Preface

Tenderness, affection, warmth, and *closeness* are words that help define intimacy. It is an extraordinary moment when we realize that someone loves us and wants an intimate relationship.

Our first experience of being loved comes from our parents. Typically, a mother's love is more obviously expressed and therefore more easily experienced. A father's love, however, is often less expressive and therefore not so easily received. To be held close by a father is a special gift. If we have not experienced that fatherly warmth, we may have a longing that is hard to replace. That longing may launch us on a search for intimacy that can sometimes end in frustration.

God knows our hearts, and He understands our need for intimacy. In His abiding love for us, He sent His Son to the cross so that we could become His. Our heavenly Father wants to be the father we long for, who loves us and holds us close.

However, we often suffer from misguided ideas of how to deepen our intimacy with God. It is easy to be like the Pharisees in thinking that if we work hard and try to be perfect, then God will accept us. It did not work for the Pharisees, and it does not work for us. The key to growing in intimacy with God is knowing that

He longs to be with us far more than we long to be with Him. We can approach Him freely, confident of His desire to hold us close.

The purpose of this devotional book is to lead you into an intimate relationship with your heavenly Father. Each of its four parts addresses a different aspect of the Father's desire for intimacy. In each part, there are seven readings so that if you choose to use it on a daily basis you can read through it in a month, exploring a different facet of intimacy each week. But the book can be read in any number of ways—daily, one part every other week, or one part a month, whatever pace meets your needs. After meditating on the primary Scripture passage and the accompanying insights, you can use the two questions following the text for reflection on the Word and in prayer. With each devotional, you will find an accompanying journal page summarizing the chapter's key thought for deeper intimacy and inviting you to record your personal thoughts about your dialogue with the Father.

I can think of no greater pursuit than intimacy with our Father. The amazing truth is that God Himself has initiated this pursuit and draws us into it. The Scriptures are filled with the Lord's expressions of desire to hold us close. If you have selected this book to read, you probably feel as I do: growing in my relationship with God has primary importance in my life. God bless you as you experience the richest and most satisfying relationship there is—intimacy with your Father.

Love in Christ,

Cynthia Heald

PART ONE

The Father's Words of Love

THE FATHER AND THE CHILD

The Father spoke:
Come, My child: I long to hold you close.

Oh, yes, Father, that is my desire also.

I know. It is your love for Me that shows Me your heart's desire to grow in intimacy.

What shall I do to draw closer to You?

I want you to learn to quiet your heart so that you can hear My voice.

How do I quiet my heart?

By being still enough to listen to My words of love. You hear so many other voices; I want you to set apart time for listening to Me.

Will this take much time?

The amount of time is not as essential as your willingness to give Me your heart.

My heart is Yours, Father.

Good. I take great pleasure in expressing My love for you.

1

You Are Mine!

But now [in spite of the past judgments for Israel's sins] thus says the Lord Who created you, O Jacob, and He Who formed You, O Israel: Fear not, for I have redeemed you—ransomed you by paying a price instead of leaving you captives; I have called you by your name, you are Mine.

—*Isaiah 43:1 AMPLIFIED*

With tears in her eyes, the young woman recounted what it was like to live with a father who was rarely involved in her life. It almost made it harder on her that he was physically present in the home because he was rarely there for her emotionally. The night of her prom, he seemed to hide behind the newspaper. He never even complimented her on her dress. Now, as an adult, she realized the implications of her loss, and she longed for the intimacy only a father can give. She wanted to know him—what he felt, what he had experienced, what he dreamed about. She needed his guidance. She felt lonely and vulnerable without the security of a father who was committed to protecting and providing for her. She yearned to be loved and accepted by the one who had given part of his life to her.

What could this young woman do? Where could she go to find such intimacy? Marriage? Close friendships?

Although love, acceptance, and sharing are elements of all intimate relationships, it is rare to experience with a husband or good friend the special dynamic of intimacy provided in the father-child relationship. A child longs to feel safe, secure, and confident in her father's unwavering love. She yearns to know that it is acceptable for her to be dependent and needy, and that her father has mature wisdom to impart to her. She needs assurance that her father loves her passionately and is committed to her forever.

Is there such a father? Does he desire intimacy? Can he love one more child? With thundering assurance our heavenly Father answers, "Come to Me. Let Me love you with an everlasting love. I desire to fulfill all your needs and to form you into a beautiful daughter who brings Me glory. Draw close to Me, and we will experience the precious gift of intimacy."

You Are Loved

When I went to college in the late fifties, a ritual between sororities and fraternities provided an opportunity for a couple to make a public declaration of their commitment to each other.

"Guess what? Jane is getting pinned to John Monday night!" you would hear as the news raced across campus. "Isn't it wonderful?"

Yes, it was wonderful. Pinning ceremonies between sororities and fraternities were always joyful and romantic occasions. On that special night, the young woman and all her sorority sisters would dress in white and stand together outside their house. The fraternity brothers would come in a group, dressed in suits and ties, with the young man carrying flowers. First the men would sing a few songs, and then the couple would meet in the middle. He would hand her the flowers, carefully affix his pin next to hers, and give her a kiss. After a few songs from the sorority, everyone would congratulate the happy couple.

It was a significant ceremony, for it was the step taken before engagement. The ritual announced to all that they were committed to each other. Everywhere the young woman went, people saw the fraternity pin she wore and knew that she was loved. Someone had said to her, "You are mine."

There is a beautiful account in Isaiah 43 of God telling Israel in front of the world, "You are Mine." The prophet recorded how God called after His wayward children, "O Jacob (supplanter!), even though I am correcting you, I want you to know that you do not need to be afraid. I will ransom you. I have called you by name. You are Mine." The Father wanted to hold Israel close to His heart. He created them from the dust of the earth, and He called them together to form them as a nation. He chose them because of His great love, and He wanted them to know they belonged to Him.

Do you long for the assurance of a father who loves you? A father who has brought you into the world, named you, and declared you to be his very own? In Ephesians 1:4 (*Message*), Paul proclaimed that what God did for Israel, He has also done for you: "Long before he laid down earth's foundations, he had us in mind, had settled on us as the focus of his love, to be made whole and holy by his love." God claims His right to be your Father by His creation of you. It was a creation planned from long ago, prompted by pure and holy love. Your heavenly Father formed you as a unique individual. You have the assurance of His constant care and presence in your life. You are His.

YOU ARE REDEEMED

What happens when a child is separated or wanders away from her father? Can she count on him to call her name, to come after her, to rescue her no matter what the danger, to pay any price to get her back?

As a young girl, I remember playing outside in the neighborhood one afternoon and then following a friend home without telling my parents that I was going to be playing inside. When they realized I was missing, both of them began looking for me. I can still hear their concerned calls, "Cynthia Ann? Cynthia Ann?" I was their child, and they were committed to finding me.

The Bible reveals a God who will go to any length to deliver His children from danger and bring them back from the consequences of their disobedience. In Isaiah 43:1, God assured Israel that He had redeemed them. The Hebrew meaning of _redeem_ is "to ransom by a price paid in lieu of the captives."[1] In this passage, God declared that He gave Egypt, Cush, and Seba as a ransom in Israel's place. The kinship was declared in His covenant with Israel: "Now then, if you will indeed obey My voice and keep My covenant, then you shall be My own possession among all the peoples, for all the earth is Mine" (Ex. 19:5 NASB). On this basis God boldly announced to His children, "I am Your Father and I have redeemed you. I want you to be My special possession, and you will be if you keep My covenant."

God's redemption of you is not in countries, but in the sacrifice of His own Son. Paul went on to proclaim in Ephesians 1:5 (_Message_), "Long, long ago he decided to adopt us into his family through Jesus Christ. (What pleasure he took in planning this!) He wanted us to enter into the celebration of his lavish gift-giving by the hand of his beloved Son."

In the Old Testament, the near relation had the right to redeem a relative in slavery or debt. Boaz did that for Ruth after her husband died. In becoming Ruth's kinsman-redeemer, Boaz accepted her as his wife. The biblical concept of redemption always implies a family relationship. God adopted you at great cost, and He thereby became your Father. Once you truly understand and accept His redemption of you, your search for a loving, protective father will be fulfilled.

God's willingness to redeem you gives Him the right of ownership, as Paul indicated when he wrote to the Corinthians, "Or do you not know that your body is a temple of the Holy Spirit who is in you, whom you have from God, and that you are not your own? For you have been bought with a price: therefore glorify God in your body" (1 Cor. 6:19–20 NASB). God has lovingly purchased you. As Boaz did with Ruth, He takes responsibility for your life—to rescue and protect you.

You Are Called by Name

When I was a child and my parents grew frustrated with something I had done—or hadn't done—they would call me by my first and middle names: "*Cynthia Ann,* come here!" Whenever they used both names, I knew they needed to talk to me about something important. When they brought me into the world and named me, in effect they proclaimed, "This is our daughter, and we are responsible for her. She is ours."

In the Hebrew culture, names carried great significance. Not only did they confer identity, but they also captured the character or reputation of the one named. For example, *Abram* means "exalted father"; *Abraham,* "father of a multitude." *Nabal* (husband of Abigail) is translated "fool." *Jesus* means "deliverer." *Jacob* means "supplanter." After Jacob wrestled with God, he was given a new name: *Israel,* "Prince with God" and "He strives with God (and prevails)." The new name was to remind the nation that there is power in prevailing prayer, and that God would fight for Israel.

When God called Israel by name, He was calling them to be His own possession. In using their given name, He affirmed their special relationship with Him. Israel would understand that because a shepherd called his own sheep by name. Therefore, Jesus used this imagery to proclaim His identity and to emphasize that we are called by name: "But he who enters by the door is a shepherd of the sheep. To him the doorkeeper opens, and the sheep hear his voice, and he calls his own sheep by name, and leads them out" (John 10:2–3 NASB).

Upon the disciples' return from their first missionary journey in amazement that the demons were subject to them, Jesus encouraged them by saying, "Nevertheless do not rejoice in this, that the spirits are subject to you, but rejoice that your names are recorded in heaven" (Luke 10:20 NASB). When I think of some of the thick phone books I have thumbed through, it is incomprehensible to conceive of a book in heaven with every believer's name written in it. Yet that is how God chooses to affirm that we are His—as individuals, gathered together in His family.

God knows your name. You are His special child, known and loved eternally by Him.

"You Are Mine!"

I never experienced my personal pinning ceremony, but I have experienced something far greater and more meaningful—the Lord's redemption and love for me. Just as He exclaimed to the Israelites, "You are Mine!" He has whispered these words in my heart too. In Isaiah, He tenderly reminded His children that He created, redeemed, and called them by name. What added assurance could He give them that He was their Father and they were His children? "We are related for all eternity! You are Mine!"

Our God is the same yesterday, today, and forever. His message of love to you is unchanging. Listen carefully to Jesus' words: "My sheep hear My voice, and I know them, and they follow Me; and I give eternal life to them, and they shall never perish; and no one shall snatch them out of My hand. My Father, who has given them to Me, is greater than all; and no one is able to snatch them out of the Father's hand. I and the Father are one" (John 10:27–30 NASB). This is the Lord's message to you. Can He speak more clearly?

> *I created you. You are My child.*
> *You are personally known and loved by Me.*
> *I have redeemed you so that we can be together always.*
> *Nothing can separate you from Me, for I am your Father.*
> *I will always hold you as close as you will let Me.*
> *You are Mine.*

With every new step we take on this journey, silently lift up to God the heart-opening reaffirmation: *Reveal truth to me. Show me how to call you Father. Draw me into your presence.*

Do you seek practicalities?

You have just prayed the most vital and practical prayer in all the universe—the prayer God longs to hear his creatures pray.

With those sixteen simple words, you have begun a quest that will change the course of your spiritual life! And as long as you continue to orient your inner being Father-ward, it is a quest that will continue to lead you to new heights, which will, in turn, open into realms of new depths of "knowing" throughout this life . . . and throughout eternity.

—Michael Phillips[2]

For Reflection

Why do you think God emphasizes in Isaiah 43:1 that He calls us by name?

Tell the Lord in prayer how you long to be held close by a loving Father.

KEY THOUGHT FOR DEEPER INTIMACY: *Because my Father has said, "You are Mine," I can be intimate with Him.*

The Father speaks *(what is He saying to you?)*:

The child responds *(what are you saying to Him?)*:

2

My Love for You Is Everlasting

Long ago the LORD said to Israel: "I have loved you, my people,
with an everlasting love. With unfailing love I have drawn you
to myself."

—*Jeremiah 31:3* NLT

One of my favorite movies is *The Princess Bride*. It tells the story
of a farm boy who falls deeply in love with the young woman he
serves. When it becomes necessary for him to leave her, they pledge
their eternal love for each other. "I will love you forever"—incredibly
beautiful words to be whispered to anyone's heart. This passionately
felt thought can be proclaimed between two people who, at the
time, sincerely do love each other. To these lovers, nothing would
ever cause them to doubt the truth of these precious words. Years
later, however, when they meet again, the young man wrongly
judges that his love has been unfaithful. He rebukes her with the
definition of *true* love: it is always steadfast and loyal, no matter
what the circumstances.

This farm boy is right about true love: it is constant and blameless. Everlasting love does not depend upon the behavior or
response of the other person. It is unchanging, permanent, strong,
trustworthy. But eternal love is rare among human beings. The
authentic, enduring love that is so necessary to our existence can be

found only in the One who *is* love, the One who has revealed Himself to be our Father.

The words that God spoke through Jeremiah, "I have loved you with an everlasting love," were a needed reminder from the heavenly Father to His children, Judah. God did not choose to declare His love at that time because His chosen were behaving righteously; they were in the midst of chastisement and exile. Because of Judah's idolatry and disobedience, they were being held captive in a foreign land. Nebuchadnezzar, the Babylonian king, had conquered Jerusalem, burned the temple and palace, and deported most of the people to Babylon.

When Judah staged a rebellion under King Zedekiah, Nebuchadnezzar was quick to lay siege to Jerusalem. Several times during the attack, Zedekiah sought Jeremiah's counsel. The king was told to surrender and it would go well with him, but he chose to turn away from the Lord's counsel and do what he thought best. The results were devastation of the city and banishment of its citizens. Zedekiah was forced to witness the slaughter of his sons and nobles. Then Nebuchadnezzar gouged out his eyes, bound him in chains, and sent him to Babylon.

Why such a severe punishment? The Scriptures tell us,

> All the leaders of the priests and the people became more and more unfaithful. They followed the pagan practices of the surrounding nations, desecrating the Temple of the LORD in Jerusalem. The LORD, the God of their ancestors, repeatedly sent his prophets to warn them, for he had compassion on his people and his Temple. But the people mocked these messengers of God and despised their words. They scoffed at the prophets until the LORD's anger could no longer be restrained and there was no remedy. (2 Chron. 36:14–16 NLT)

Now, with His children in the process of being disciplined, God spoke of His love:

Why do you protest your punishment—this wound that has no cure? I have had to punish you because your sins are many and your guilt is great . . . But the LORD says this: When I bring you home again from your captivity and restore your fortunes, Jerusalem will be rebuilt on her ruins. The palace will be reconstructed as it was before. There will be joy and songs of thanksgiving, and I will multiply my people and make of them a great and honored nation . . . You will be my people, and I will be your God . . . I have loved you, my people, with an everlasting love. With unfailing love I have drawn you to myself. (Jer. 30:15, 18–19, 22; 31:3 NLT)

These amazing words from God reveal His character and desire to love all His children with an infinite love—a love that is unconditional, independent of our actions or worthiness. He bestows upon His children an enduring love because He considers us worth loving.

Why should the Father love children who are so prone to sin? Why does He pour out His love on us, who are not prone to return that love unless we think it is to our advantage?

He Loves Us No Matter What

Our worthiness or goodness is irrelevant to God's decision to love us. The nation Judah, having forsaken the Lord for idols, was certainly not worthy to continue to receive God's grace and love. Nevertheless, in the midst of the people's disobedience, He comforted and consoled them, reminding them of His unchanging love.

I will never forget one instance in which, after being with a group of people, I felt that I had not shown love or grace. I left feeling totally inadequate to be called His child. As I was confessing and conversing with the Lord, the one predominant impression in my heart was this: *Cynthia, I love you. I know you are not perfect, but I love you deeply. You are My child.*

The Lord continues to speak to His own of His consistent love even when we are not at all lovable.

The young man in *The Princess Bride* was ready to condemn his true love and leave her when he thought she had been unfaithful. If a loved one breaks faith, we feel justified in withdrawing our love. But God's ways are not our ways. When the people of Judah turned their backs on God and instead worshiped the detestable Baal, God mercifully chastised them, but He was faithful to remain their Father. "God is no respecter of persons, but will show his hatred of sin wherever he finds it," observed Matthew Henry, "and that he hates it most in those that are nearest to him."[1]

Through Abraham, God made a covenant with Israel that He would be their God. His word is sacred. His love is not impulsive. It was proclaimed from the beginning of His relationship with His people, and it will never change. His faithfulness to His pledge does not depend on His children's faithfulness. He is faithful to correct, as a loving father should, but He is also faithful to restore and to provide continual assurance of His unfailing love.

Because the Father's love is everlasting, He will continue extending, continue drawing out at length, His loving-kindness. In this context, Jeremiah 29:11 (NLT) has new meaning: "'For I know the plans I have for you,' says the LORD. 'They are plans for good and not for disaster, to give you a future and a hope.'" His *good* plans for His children spring from His everlasting love.

My love is not everlasting. My love is conditional and intermittent. I enjoy loving my family and friends and doing things for them when they appreciate me and show me their love. But I am tempted to distance myself from them if I sense they are too busy or preoccupied to want me in their lives. Not our Father—He loves us when we turn away, when we forget Him, when we think we don't need His love.

The apostle Paul understood God's eternal love well when he wrote, "I am convinced that nothing can ever separate us from his love" (Rom. 8:38 NLT). Knowing that God's love is unfailing, that

His commitment is eternal, that nothing can separate us, gives us security and freedom in seeking intimacy with our Father. In declaring His constant, unconditional, abiding love, God wants us to understand the depth of His desire to hold us close. And so, independent of our character or circumstances, He continually says, "I love you, Judah. I love you, Zedekiah. I love *you*, My child, with an everlasting love."

> It is, indeed, a marvel that, through these long ages of the world's wild wanderings, God should still follow his unworthy children with ceaseless love, never refusing to bless them, always entreating them to return to him . . . It is the nature of true and perfect love to be eternal.
>
> —W. F. Adeney[2]

For Reflection

How do the Father's words in Jeremiah 31:3 compare or contrast with your experience of love?

In prayer, respond to God's tender declaration of His love for you.

KEY THOUGHT FOR DEEPER INTIMACY: *Because my Father has declared His everlasting love to me, I know He will always hold me close when I approach Him.*

The Father speaks *(what is He saying to you?)*:

The child responds *(what are you saying to Him?)*:

3

I Am the One Who Leads You

"Come near to Me, hear this:
I have not spoken in secret from the beginning;
From the time that it was, I was there.
And now the LORD God and His Spirit
Have sent Me."
Thus says the LORD, your Redeemer,
The Holy One of Israel:
"I am the LORD your God,
Who teaches you to profit,
Who leads you by the way you should go."

—*Isaiah 48:16–17* NKJV

*M*rs. Badolett was my sixth-grade teacher. Even though almost half a century has gone by, I still remember her striking gray hair, her colorful clothes with matching shoes, and the way she always stood erect, commanding attention and respect. But most of all, I remember the joy she took in teaching.

Mrs. Badolett had the ability to vary our subjects in clever, creative ways. I don't ever remember being bored. My favorite time of the day was after lunch. Each day she read to us a chapter from a classic book. *The Secret Garden* was my favorite. I was blessed to have such a special teacher who would place her hand on my shoulder, look me in the eye, and inspire me to excel—to read, to learn, to explore. She was the only teacher I ever went back to visit. She influenced my life for good.

This is the mission of a good teacher: to influence, train, and equip a child to appreciate fully all that is good, and to cultivate a desire to be taught. Few teachers have the gift of motivating a student to listen, trust, and obey. But as rare as such a teacher is, she can never impart the priceless wisdom we can learn only at the feet of our Lord. Although we may be fortunate to have spiritual mentors, Bible teachers, and books that can guide and teach us, the Father is the only One who can hold us close in intimate love when we go to Him to be taught.

What a privilege it is to receive instruction from the Lord: He who is Wisdom itself. The passage in Isaiah 48:16–17 speaks of the Messiah. He invites you to come near and listen. He speaks clearly as your Redeemer and Lord in revealing His desire to teach you and lead you.

WHAT HE WANTS US TO HEAR

To learn from the Lord, we need to start with a heart willing to obey what we hear. In Isaiah 48:18 (NKJV), the Lord laments,

> Oh, that you had heeded My commandments!
> Then your peace would have been like a river,
> And your righteousness like the waves of the sea.

After I graduated from college, I taught high school English. I was very young. Without Mrs. Badolett's gray hair it was hard for me to establish credibility and command the students' undivided attention. It was frustrating to teach while knowing that much of it was falling on deaf ears (although the hearing ratio did increase after the first test) because so many of the students clearly had no intention of learning or doing what was asked.

My teaching was academic; the Lord schools us in life. Despite His life-changing teaching, however, He encounters the same hearing problem with some of His children. His true, pure, and profitable words fall on deaf ears if there is not a heart willing to obey. We have already seen what happened to Zedekiah when he did not listen to and heed the Lord's counsel through Jeremiah.

So the Lord emphasizes in His Word through Isaiah, "Come near to Me, hear this . . ." And what does He want to teach us? That He is the Lord our God.

Another way of phrasing Jesus' statement to His disciples, "I am the vine; you are the branches" (John 15:5 NLT), would be, "I am the teacher; you are the students. When I speak, please listen and do what I say." How patient of the Lord to remind us that He is our Father, our Redeemer, our Teacher, our Guide, and that we are His children. I smile whenever I read Jesus' explanation of the vine and the branches because even after three years of ministry together, He had to remind His disciples of who He was and who they were in relation to Him: "I am the LORD your God."

When I was in my mid-twenties, through a series of hard circumstances the Lord first whispered to my heart: *Cynthia, since I am the Lord your God, let Me be the Lord to you personally. I am your Father and you are My child, and I want our relationship to be the best that it can be. I love you and I want to be able to hold you close— all the time.* I knew what He was asking of me: that I surrender my life to Him.

As I pondered the request from the Lord, I thought, *He is right! He is the Lord, my Redeemer, the Holy One of Israel. Why not let Him have His rightful place in my life? Why should I be so presumptuous to think that I, a child, would know more than my Father?* At the time, although I was living my life as best I could, I was weary and discouraged. *Yes, Lord, You can have my life,* I told Him.

When Job was brought to a point of utter surrender to God, he was ready to hear and obey whatever God imparted to him. After God spoke to him out of the whirlwind, Job responded,

> I know that Thou canst do all things,
> And that no purpose of Thine can be thwarted . . .
> Hear, now, and I will speak;
> I will ask Thee, and do Thou instruct me. (Job 42:2, 4 NASB)

Job's whole relationship with the Lord changed. Instead of demanding that God answer him, Job humbly repented. From then on, he would only be instructed. God became the Lord his God. Job echoed the good words of the young man Samuel, "Speak, Lord, for Your servant is listening."

What does the Lord our God want to teach you? He wants to instruct you in what is good, what is profitable. Isaiah 48:17 (NKJV) says that God teaches us "to profit." *Profit* means "gain, advantage, welfare, benefit, usefulness, improvement, fruitfulness." As a faithful teacher, God wants to teach you what is good for you. God is *for* you, as Paul indicated in Romans 8:31–32 (NLT): "If God is for us, who can ever be against us? Since God did not spare even his own Son but gave him up for us all, won't God, who gave us Christ, also give us everything else?"

What He Knows Is Good for Us

What is good from God's viewpoint is Christlikeness, the fruit of the Spirit. He teaches you so that you may learn the value and profitability of the eternal. You are now His child. You are no longer to seek satisfaction from the world. Your joy will come from close, abiding fellowship with your Father as you fulfill His purposes for you.

God is continually creative in the ways He challenges me to stop holding on to the temporal and let go of *my* way of doing things. One of these ways has been the experience of having others stay in our home when we are traveling. Those who stay in our home are always careful to be good stewards and to keep the house clean. Inevitably, though, things are not always put back in the right place, and sometimes they get broken. At those times the Lord gently instructs me, *Cynthia, whose home is this? Is it yours to cling to and zealously guard? Or is it Mine to be used to serve others?*

How easily we are deceived by what *we* think is good and profitable. For instance, I think it is good not to have any trials! But God, who desires us to become like His Son, uses affliction for our profit. There are some types of suffering we will never understand, such as disease, fatal accidents, and natural disasters. But this is where our faith in the everlasting love of God is crucial. We have the promise of His amazing ability to work all things together for our ultimate good: the fruit of godly living, which brings Him praise and glory.

Trials and suffering are givens in our world. Jesus said that in the world, we will have troubles. But some of our trials are consequences of our determination to live on our own terms. Judah was in exile because it chose to turn away from the Lord. God emphatically stated in Isaiah 48:18 that if His children had obeyed His commands, peace and righteousness would have been their reward.

Matthew Henry makes clear that when we submit to God's instruction through the tribulations of life, we receive the good that He wants for us:

> By this God shows himself to be a God in covenant with us, by his teaching us; and none teaches like him, for he gives an understanding. Whom God redeems he teaches; whom he designs to deliver out of their afflictions he first teaches to profit by their afflictions, makes them partakers of his holiness, for that is the profit for which he chastens us.[1]

What is the lesson for the student? Listen to the Lord with a heart to obey!

The Lord wants not only to teach you, but also to guide you in the way you should go. He has "a way" for you. Generally, for all His children, His desired path is one of intimacy and holiness. Specifically, He leads as you surrender control of your life and take hold of His hand so that He can guide you in the way He has for you personally.

When the Lord asked me to surrender, He also said, *Cynthia, come, take My hand and walk with Me the rest of your life.* He didn't tell me where we were going; all I knew was that I wanted to go with Him. It didn't matter where the path led. All I wanted was my Father to be my guide.

How blessed you are to have a Father who cares enough to accompany you on your journey and teach and guide you along the way. May you become very close and intimate with your wonderful Counselor, your Redeemer, the Holy One of Israel: your Lord and your God.

God never speaks to us in startling ways, but in ways that are easy to misunderstand, and we say, "I wonder if that is God's voice?" Isaiah said that the Lord spake to him "with a strong hand," that is, by the pressure of circumstances. Nothing touches our lives but it is God Himself speaking. Do we discern His hand or only mere occurrence?

Get into the habit of saying "Speak, Lord," and life will become a romance. Every time circumstances press, say, "Speak, Lord"; make time to listen. Chastening is more than a means of discipline, it is meant to get me to the place of saying, "Speak, Lord."

—Oswald Chambers[2]

For Reflection

What areas of your life will change as you allow your heavenly Father to teach and lead you according to His promise in Isaiah 48:16–17?

Speak to the Lord about your desire to experience His instruction and leading in your life.

KEY THOUGHT FOR DEEPER INTIMACY: *My Father draws near to me when I take His hand and say, "Speak, Lord."*

The Father speaks *(what is He saying to you?):*

The child responds *(what are you saying to Him?):*

4

You Have the Right to Be My Child

As many as received Him, to them He gave the right to become children of God, to those who believe in His name: who were born, not of blood, nor of the will of the flesh, nor of the will of man, but of God.

—*John 1:12–13* NKJV

If you were sent to a deserted island and could take only three books, which ones would you choose?" When I was asked this question during a small group meeting, I knew immediately how I would answer: my Bible, Oswald Chambers's *My Utmost for His Highest,* and Jane Austen's novel *Pride and Prejudice.* I could not live without God's Word to teach me, encourage me, and change me. Oswald Chambers's insightful writings continually minister to me and challenge me in my walk with God. Jane Austen's wonderful observations on human relations and society provide continual enjoyment.

As I was meditating on the concept of lineage in John 1:12, I was reminded of a scene in *Pride and Prejudice.* In a spirited conversation, Lady Catherine de Bourgh challenges Elizabeth Bennet concerning a report that she and Mr. Darcy, her rich nephew, are to be wed. This idea appalls Her Ladyship, in no small measure because of Elizabeth's lack of family and social "connections." Lady Catherine admonishes Elizabeth, "The upstart pretensions of a young woman without family, connections, or fortune. Is this to be endured? . . . Who was your mother? Who are your aunts and uncles?"[1]

We all know that prejudice of this kind is not limited to characters in novels! "Who are your parents? What do they do? Where do you live? Where do you work?" These are common questions often asked to determine exactly where someone might be on the social scale.

Those who have received the Lord and believe in His name can offer this response when asked about their family connections: "I have an impeccable heritage and excellent lineage. I am a child of the God of the universe, born according to His will. He calls me by name, loves me with an everlasting love, guides me, and cares deeply for me."

BELIEVING AND RECEIVING

What does it mean to receive the Lord? *Receive* means "to accept, embrace, follow, agree with, welcome." When you encounter Christ, you can receive Him or reject Him. In the verses leading up to John 1:12, we learn that although Christ was in the world, and the world was made through Him, the world did not know Him.

It seems understandable that the world would fail to recognize Christ, but it is surprising to learn that when He came to His own people, Israel, they did not receive Him: "He came to His own, and His own did not receive Him" (John 1:11 NKJV). It wasn't so much that Israel didn't *know* the Lord, because they had been given many prophecies concerning the coming Messiah, and Jesus taught with authority, performed miracles, and fulfilled all that His Father purposed for Him. Yet His own people did not welcome Him. They refused to receive Him.

Because members of the Jewish establishment were unwilling to embrace Jesus, they certainly did not believe in His name. Actually, *to believe* is a good explanation of what it means *to receive*. I have not really received a truth until I believe—"trust, rely on, have confidence in, am persuaded, have faith"—in that truth. The belief that is necessary to become a child of God is complete trust *in His name*.

As John began his gospel, he presented Jesus as the Word, the *Logos:* the full revelation of the essence, character, and activity of God.[2] Matthew Henry explained what it means to believe in Christ's name:

> His name is *the Word of God; the King of kings, the Lord our righteousness; Jesus our Savior.* Now to believe on his name is to acknowledge that he is what these great names bespeak him to be, and to acquiesce in it, that he may be so to us . . . Believing in Christ's name is *receiving* him as a gift from God. We must receive his doctrine as true and good; receive his law as just and holy; receive his offers as kind and advantageous; and we must receive the image of his grace, and impressions of his love, as the governing principle of our affections and actions.[3]

When the angel appeared to Joseph, Mary's betrothed, he told Joseph to name the baby Jesus, or *Yeshua,* which means "the Lord shall save."[4] To believe in the name of Jesus is to accept Him as the Son of God, my Savior, my Redeemer. It is to acknowledge my sin and admit my need for a Savior. It is to believe that Christ's death on the cross paid the penalty for my sin. By receiving Him into my heart and life, I become a child of God.

As a girl of twelve, I remember the Lord's touch on my heart when I was asked in church, "Do you believe that Jesus Christ is the Son of God and that He died for your sins?" My positive answer was not simply a statement of belief, but an act of acceptance. It was then that I became His child. I received; I believed; I welcomed the Lord Jesus into my life.

The apostle John went on to explain what it means to believe and receive: "They are reborn! This is not a physical birth resulting from human passion or plan—this rebirth comes from God" (1:13 NLT). In the past, God had announced, "Israel is My son, My firstborn" (Ex. 4:22 NKJV). God had chosen the nation of Israel to be

His child. In sending His Son, the Father was choosing to adopt all who believe.

Natural birth is the beginning of physical life; rebirth from God is the beginning of spiritual life. Our natural birth results from the will of the flesh. Our spiritual birth is the supernatural work of the will of God. In the past, we were slaves to sin. Rebirth frees us from the bondage of sin. We have turned from darkness to light, from the power of Satan to the power of God. The old life is gone. The new life has come! All of this happens only by God's regeneration through the power of the Holy Spirit.

In the course of Jesus' conversation with the Pharisee Nicodemus, Jesus told him that he must be born again: "The truth is, no one can enter the Kingdom of God without being born of water and the Spirit. Humans can reproduce only human life, but the Holy Spirit gives new life from heaven" (John 3:5–6 NLT).

Like Lady Catherine de Bourgh, the Pharisees gloried in their ancestry. As Jews, they felt they should receive special honor because of their noble blood and parentage. John recorded an interesting exchange between Jesus and the Pharisees in which Jesus rebuked them for following their father, the devil. They shouted back at Him, "Our father is Abraham." Jesus replied that the children of Abraham would not try to kill Him. The Pharisees, always conscious of heritage, bitingly replied, "We were not born out of wedlock! Our true Father is God himself" (John 8:34–41 NLT). What pride and prejudice!

The Pharisees were deceived in their presumption that religious heritage automatically qualified them as children of God. That is why the Scripture so clearly states that our rebirth has absolutely nothing to do with any human endeavor. As we truly grasp that our spiritual birth is adoption by our heavenly Father, solely because of His grace, we will be overwhelmed by the love of

God. Here is irrefutable proof of His abundant loving-kindness, lavished on believing hearts.

As God's children, we have incredible privileges: eternal life, an eternal home, everlasting love, our Father's own nature, a new family—relatives who might even satisfy Lady Catherine! "See how very much our heavenly Father loves us, for he allows us to be called his children, and we really are!" (1 John 3:1 NLT).

When our youngest son, Michael, was born, his older brother and sisters (Daryl, Melinda, and Shelly) came to the hospital with Jack, my husband, to take us home. I will never forget Jack's glowing countenance in the elevator as he held Michael while the other three stood around his legs. There was such a look of joy and pride as he stood there surrounded by his children. His broad smile to everyone he encountered communicated, "These are my children. I am their father, and I love them with all my heart."

These are the very thoughts of your heavenly Father, who is saying to you, "I am your Father, and you are My child. I love you with all My heart."

> He is born of the spirit and has become a legitimate child of God. He has "partaken of the divine nature" and Christ is begotten in him "the hope of glory." As he is a child of God, he is also "heir of God, and a joint-heir with Jesus Christ." The new divine nature is more deeply implanted in his being than the human nature of his earthly father or mother.
>
> —Lewis Sperry Chafer[5]

For Reflection

Based on John 1:12–13, how do you perceive your relationship with God?

Respond in prayer to your Father's declaration that He has given you the right to become His beloved child.

KEY THOUGHT FOR DEEPER INTIMACY: *I know that in receiving and believing Christ, I become God's dearly loved child.*

The Father speaks *(what is He saying to you?)*:

The child responds *(what are you saying to Him?)*:

5

Seek First
My Kingdom

Therefore do not worry and be anxious, saying, What are we
going to have to eat? or, What are we going to have to drink? Or,
What are we going to have to wear? For the Gentiles (heathen)
wish for and crave and diligently seek after all these things; and
your heavenly Father well knows that you need them all. But
seek for (aim at and strive after) first of all His kingdom, and His
righteousness [His way of doing and being right], and then all
these things taken together will be given you besides.

—*Matthew 6:31–33* AMPLIFIED

*H*ave you ever read these words of Jesus recorded in Matthew 6
and thought to yourself, *This really doesn't make a whole lot of sense.
Of course I have to be concerned about having food to eat and clothes
to wear. If I don't worry about these essentials, who will? God isn't going
to supply these needs supernaturally; I have to do my part. What about
the Proverbs 31 woman? She worked hard spinning wool and flax. She
provided food for her family. She even planted a vineyard! She made
sure that all in her household were properly clothed, and she wore lovely
dresses. Was she wrong to do those things?*

Let's look more closely at what Jesus says. In Matthew 6:19, He
teaches that we should be more concerned with storing eternal treasures in heaven than with accumulating temporal wealth here on

earth, which will perish. John echoed the teaching when he wrote, "Stop loving this evil world and all that it offers you, for when you love the world, you show that you do not have the love of the Father in you. For the world offers only the lust for physical pleasure, the lust for everything we see, and pride in our possessions" (1 John 2:15–16 NLT).

Jesus does not tell us to forget about the necessities of life. He is more concerned with what we value as most important: "Wherever your treasure is, there your heart and thoughts will also be . . . No one can serve two masters. For you will hate one and love the other, or be devoted to one and despise the other. You cannot serve both God and money" (Matt. 6:21, 24 NLT). Jesus wants us to understand that our outlook on life should be focused on the eternal, the priceless treasures of God, not on the temporal, the superficial things of the world.

WHAT PREOCCUPIES YOUR ATTENTION?

Why do you get up in the morning? Are your initial thoughts about everything that needs to be done so that you and your family can survive? Or do you wake up thinking about seeking the kingdom of God and His righteousness? What preoccupies your attention?

Because we are God's children, our primary desire and concern should be for Him. To *seek* first His kingdom and righteousness means to "pursue, yearn for, desire, dig for, research." I frequently misplace my glasses (a sure sign of old age!). When they are missing, I turn my attention to searching for them until I find them because I really can't do anything without them. My pursuit of the things of God should be conducted with at least the same diligence I expend in seeking an object that is valuable to me.

In pursuing the kingdom of God, we are seeking to remain within the realm of God's rule and to develop the character that results from this search. I seek first His kingdom to have His will in my life and to have a part in the expansion of His kingdom. I need to be diligent in seeking to become a worthy citizen of His kingdom, exemplified by my character and conduct. In seeking first His kingdom, I store treasures in heaven.

Jesus reiterated the high priority of seeking the eternal over the temporal in His encounter with Martha during His dinner visit to her home. She grew so anxious about preparing food and sitting down to eat that she mildly rebuked the Lord for failing to send her sister, Mary, into the kitchen to help her. Jesus answered her, "My dear Martha, you are so upset over all these details! There is really only one thing worth being concerned about. Mary has discovered it—and I won't take it away from her" (Luke 10:41–42 NLT). His reply to Martha is a charge to all of us: there is only *one* thing! You must not be anxious about temporal matters. You must seek *first* My kingdom, as Mary has done. She has been sitting at My feet, listening to My words. Her attention is preoccupied with spiritual food. Trust Me. I am perfectly capable of providing all that we need for dinner.

It is all too easy to become distracted, like Martha, by concerns over the physical aspects of life. We can allow ourselves to become so anxious that the necessities tend to dominate our days and steal away any time we might spend in seeking His kingdom. Jesus provided a picture of where these distractions lead in His parable of the sower: "The thorny ground represents those who hear and accept the Good News, but all too quickly the message is crowded out by the cares of this life, the lure of wealth, and the desire for nice things, so no crop is produced" (Mark 4:18–19 NLT). Are you able to sit at His feet consistently, reading and listening to His words? Do you spend time in His presence each day? Or is your time consumed by the cares of this life?

TRUSTING IN HIS PROVISION

Jesus teaches that our heavenly Father already knows our needs, and He will provide for them when we trust Him and live for Him.

When I was a young child, I never worried about having enough food to eat even though we lived through food-rationing measures during World War II. I had a child's simple trust that my parents would provide. So it must be with God's children. Nothing is impossible for our heavenly Father. He has instructed us to be concerned about only one thing: drawing closer to Him. As we seek Him and spend time with Him, sitting at His feet, He delights in providing all that we need for each day.

After Solomon led the leaders of Israel in worshiping the Lord, God appeared to him in a dream and asked the future king what he wanted. Solomon answered as one who was seeking God's kingdom above all else: "Give me wisdom and knowledge to rule them properly, for who is able to govern this great nation of yours?" (2 Chron. 1:10 NLT). God was pleased with Solomon's request because he did not seek anything temporal or material. In response, God told Solomon that not only would He give him wisdom and knowledge, but He would also provide riches (food, clothing, shelter) and honor.

Jesus' teaching to seek His kingdom above all else runs entirely against the grain of our culture and way of thinking. We have no problem with how busy the Proverbs 31 woman was. Yes, she provided food, drink, and clothing. She was diligent to fulfill her God-given roles. But the key to her life was not her efforts to provide for her family; it was her identity as a woman who feared God. She was outstanding in her virtuous character, her wise words, her kindness, and her sacrificial service to others. Fearing God means letting the daily concerns of life take their place behind seeking Him above all else and giving Him the rightful place in our lives.

Jesus did not say to His disciples, "Don't eat, drink, or wear clothes." He said, "Do not worry and be anxious." He reminded us that our heavenly Father provides even for the birds of the air, and we are far more valuable to Him. Jesus wants us to understand that life consists of much more than physical existence.

In 1977, our family took a leap of faith. Jack sold his veterinary practice, and we moved with our four children from San Antonio,

Texas, to Tucson, Arizona. We did that in order to minister with the Navigators, a lay ministry that emphasizes helping others navigate their way through life as committed disciples. Since the organization is a faith ministry, our move meant transitioning from a business income to the support of gifts from people who wanted to help us minister to others.

It was particularly hard for my dad to see us go with no visible means of support. After the necessary paperwork was accomplished, my dad handed me a checkbook. "I want you to take this," he said. "And if you need anything, I want you to write a check. I don't ever want you to lack for anything." I hugged my dad, but I never used his checks. I didn't need to. I had a heavenly Father who had already said the same thing to me.

Are you preoccupied with the day-to-day necessities of life? There is so much more that our Father has to give you—spiritual food, grace, guidance, love. You are His child, and He takes full responsibility for your life. All He asks is that you trust Him and make Him your main pursuit in life. Seek Him first, and you will experience His love.

> He bids us trust in God with quiet faith; he will give us food and raiment who feeds the ravens when they cry, and adorns the lilies of the field with brilliant colour . . . He knoweth our needs; he bids us ask him for our daily bread; he listens to our prayer. His children must not be like the heathen. They have far higher privileges; they must live a higher life. The heathen seek eagerly after the good things of this world; Christians must "seek first the kingdom of God and his righteousness"— that kingdom of grace in the heart, which is "righteousness and peace and joy in the Holy Ghost." That must be the first and paramount object of the Christian's hope and earnest effort; the glad submission of his whole heart, with all its fears and hopes, all its joys and sorrows, all its desires and all its thoughts, to the heavenly King, who would make that heart

his dwelling-place, reigning there with undivided sovereignty. Seek that first, above all things else—above riches, honour, comfort, ease, even above the love of those who are nearest and dearest. Seek that first, seek it of God with unresting, unwearied energy of supplication; and for other things trust his love.

—B. C. Caffin[1]

For Reflection

Reflect on Jesus' words in Matthew 6:31–33. Imagine two women: one who trusts in her heavenly Father's provision, and one who is not aware of her Father's care. How would their lives differ?

Tell your Father what anxieties you need to lay aside in order to trust His provision for you.

[handwritten] • interview tomorrow
↳ Lord God, I pray you can be revealed through me, that I present myself as the best I can be—that they can see my strengths and if this position is right for me. Please prepare my heart for your answer. Let me not be discouraged.

KEY THOUGHT FOR DEEPER INTIMACY: *When I seek my Father's kingdom and righteousness, He frees me from anxiety and draws me closer to Him.*

The Father speaks *(what is He saying to you?)*:

The child responds *(what are you saying to Him?)*:

6

I Dwell with the Humble

Thus says the High and Lofty One
Who inhabits eternity, whose name is Holy:
"I dwell in the high and holy place,
With him who has a contrite and humble spirit,
To revive the spirit of the humble,
And to revive the heart of the contrite ones."

—*Isaiah 57:15* NKJV

*P*lace yourself with Isaiah as he gazed upon a vision of the glorious splendor of God:

> I saw the Lord sitting on a throne, high and lifted up, and the train of His robe filled the temple. Above it stood seraphim; each one had six wings . . . And one cried to another and said:
>
> "Holy, holy, holy is the LORD of hosts;
> The whole earth is full of His glory!"
>
> And the posts of the door were shaken by the voice of him who cried out, and the house was filled with smoke. (Isa. 6:1–4 NKJV)

Can you imagine experiencing such a remarkable display? Most kings wore flowing robes, and Solomon's throne was high—six steps up from the floor. But no earthly king had so lofty and elaborate a throne; no earthly king had robes that completely filled the room; no earthly king had heavenly beings hovering around him, gloriously singing and praising his holiness and majesty.

That was the amazing vision Isaiah had in mind when he penned the passage in 57:15, announcing God's choice to dwell with the humble and contrite. As the Holy Spirit moved Isaiah to write, the prophet must have stopped when he revisited the encounter he recorded in chapter 6. As the extraordinary vision became new again, it would envelop him in the glory and exaltation of his God. He had to pause, drop his pen, close his eyes, and picture once more the awesome beauty of the High and Lofty One—the most high and most exalted Being in the universe.

Truly, God is far above anything we can ever conceive. For as high as the heavens are above the earth, so are His ways and His thoughts above ours (Isa. 55:9). He is King of kings and Lord of lords. He inhabits eternity, a place where time is unknown. There is no beginning of days or end of life for Him. He is not bound by time: "A day is like a thousand years [to Him], and a thousand years is like a day" (2 Peter 3:8 NLT). He is from everlasting to everlasting. This transcendence of time enables Him to give individual time to each of His children.

The seraphim continually proclaimed God "holy, holy, holy." Holiness describes His perfection of character—His thoughts, acts, and words are wholly pure and excellent. He is the only One who merits this praise:

> There is no attribute so essential to God as this. It is for his holiness, more than for anything else, that his creatures worship him. The triple repetition has been understood in all ages of the Church as connected with the doctrine of the Trinity. Holy is he who created us, and bidden us worship him in the beauty of

holiness! Holy is he who has redeemed us, and washed away our sins, and made us by profession holy! Holy is he who day by day sanctifies us, and makes us in very deed and truth, so far as we will permit him, holy![1]

TRADING THE HOLY ONE FOR IDOLS

What an awesome God—He is highly exalted, holy, eternal, and incomparable. Apparently, though, Israel would not agree. We find this rebuke to Israel in the book of Isaiah: "You worship your idols with great passion beneath every green tree. You slaughter your children as human sacrifices down in the valleys, under overhanging rocks. Your gods are the smooth stones in the valleys. You worship them with drink offerings and grain offerings. They, not I, are your inheritance" (57:5–6 NLT).

How could the Israelites turn their backs on the High and Lofty One? How could they trade Him for a stone or a piece of carved wood and worship that instead? Why did the High and Lofty One, who inhabits eternity, have to compete with inanimate, man-made idols?

Why does God have to keep repeating over and over again to us: I am the High and Lofty One; seek Me first; love Me with all your heart?

Perhaps Israel's problem is ours as well. The Israelites had turned away from God and begun to rely on their own insight. They felt they had to have the help of foreign powers rather than God's strength and protection. They found more gratification in worshiping man-made gods, inanimate objects they could see and touch, than the invisible but living God. They actually thought that the idols could help them, and they were unwilling to return to God.

This problem is as old as Adam and Eve. By yielding to the temptation of eating the forbidden fruit, they essentially told God, "We are no longer bound by Your laws. We know what is best, and we will act accordingly." This pride grieves the heart of God. It is sin, and it separates His children from Him.

In the face of His children's arrogance, God made an incredible pronouncement: He still wanted to have a relationship with His children. Since they would not come to Him, He would go to them.

THE PLACE WHERE GOD DWELLS

When Isaiah saw God in all His splendor, his immediate response was recognition of his own impurity in the face of such glory: "I am a sinful man and a member of a sinful race" (6:5 NLT). When we behold God as He truly is—the only true God, the only One worthy of our worship—we are moved to humility and repentance: "You are almighty God, and I have fallen short of Your glory." This statement pleases God because it grants Him the honor and homage due His name.

Acknowledging our sinfulness in light of God's holiness is a condition for fellowship with Him. It is the posture of a contrite and humble spirit. Contrition is the antithesis of pride. A contrite spirit arises from a broken heart, crushed by its sense of sin and unworthiness. The prideful heart is far from broken. It is consumed with self, as exemplified by Eve's response: "I want this fruit! I know what is best!" A prideful heart is insensitive to sin and therefore unaware of any need for humility. In contrast, a contrite heart recognizes the arrogance of presuming that self can take the place of God.

As we approach our Father with humility and reverence, we call forth His mercy and grace. He responds tenderly to our acceptance of who He is and who we are. He promises to dwell with His children who understand the need for a holy God. How remarkable that we should become the place where God dwells! "The heaven of heavens is not too great for him, and a human heart is not too small for him, to dwell in."[2] What phenomenal condescension and humility it shows in God's character that He would come "down" to our level to abide with us. It is His way of writing His law in our hearts. When His Spirit is within us, we are able to obey Him. When we obey Him, we enjoy sweet intimacy with Him.

God's invasion of our hearts produces spiritual life and comfort. His desire is "to revive the spirit of the humble" (Isa. 57:15 NKJV). *To revive the spirit* literally means "to make alive."[3] The New Living Translation reads, "I refresh the humble and give new courage to those with repentant hearts" (Isa. 57:15 NLT). How can a dead idol refresh, give courage, or renew a heart? Only our high and lofty God can comfort and heal and bring to life as He works in us through His Word and His Spirit. We fall down before Him broken and crushed by sin, but He speaks loving words to us and binds up our broken hearts. We rise refreshed and revived. This is what a loving Father does for His children.

I remember attending a women's conference that featured a speaker whom I held in high esteem. I wanted to meet her, but my natural intimidation around well-known people made me hesitate. I never seem to know what to say or how to approach individuals I have admired from a distance.

I finally mustered the courage to go up to the woman, introduce myself, and ask if we could spend a little time together. She was very gracious in assenting, and now we have a friendship. In order for me to make contact with her, however, I had to humble myself. I had to put aside my prideful self-consciousness and be vulnerable enough to take the risk that she might decline a meeting. I'm so glad that I didn't withhold myself in pride because I would have missed out on a valuable friendship.

So it is with our Father. Your willingness to humble yourself is essential to receiving this precious relationship. Isaiah's beautiful words of love are spoken to you from your Father. He desires to dwell with you, revive you, and share His life with you. The fellowship and refreshment offered by our holy God will bring you joy, now and forever.

One thing alone, dear Lord! I dread;—
To have a secret spot
That separates my soul from Thee,
And yet to know it not.

—Frederick W. Faber[4]

For Reflection

In Isaiah 57:15, why do you think God speaks of His high and holy character in contrast to His descent to dwell among the humble and contrite?

Come before your Father with a humble and contrite spirit, and express your longing for Him to dwell within your heart.

KEY THOUGHT FOR DEEPER INTIMACY: *My Father embraces me when I am sorrowful over sin and stand in awe of His holiness.*

The Father speaks *(what is He saying to you?)*:

The child responds *(what are you saying to Him?)*:

7

I Will Deliver You

Because he has set his love upon Me, therefore I will deliver him;
I will set him on high, because he has known My name.

—*Psalm 91:14 NKJV*

The exceptional movie *The Seven Samurai* dramatizes the story of a small village threatened by a band of thieves who want to conquer and control its inhabitants. The villagers are poor farmers who are used to living simply and peacefully. Their work is strenuous, but they are basically content. Since they are not capable of defending themselves, they seek the protection of brave samurai warriors to ward off the attack.

The movie depicts the long and painstaking process of finding someone to defend the village. It is not easy to find individuals willing to sacrifice their time, and possibly their lives, to fight someone else's battles.

Samurai, knights on white horses, brave defenders—they often seem limited to fictional stories in movies or books. There is one book, however, that tells of a true-life defender who is always ready to protect and deliver. This defender, if sought, will be found; if called upon, will answer; if needed, will rescue. He is the perfect deliverer—He is our Father.

As Psalm 91:14 indicates, *setting* your love upon the Lord is the basis for His commitment to deliver you. Setting your love upon someone means that your love is fixed, constant, immovable, permanent.

The parable of the prodigal son illustrates a father's inability to help his son when his son's love was not *set* on him. The son demanded his inheritance, left his father, journeyed to a far country, and lived recklessly. After spending all his money and encountering a severe famine, he was left destitute and starving. At that point he realized that even his father's hired servants were better off than he was because they had bread to eat. He returned to his father, who welcomed him lavishly and delivered him from his trouble.

When the son left, turned his back on his father, and *removed* his love, the father was unable to help his son. It was only when the prodigal returned that his father could embrace and refresh him. His son's love was once again *set* upon him.

The love that is "set" is a special love. "The verb used here for *love* is not the usual Hebrew word for love. It has the idea of 'holding close to,' even 'hugging tightly in love.'"[1] This love implies the strongest attachment and can be compared to our phrase "to fall in love." The source of this warm love is the heart, and its attraction is the beauty of the Lord.[2]

Mary Magdalene epitomized this kind of devotion to the Lord. Deeply grateful for her physical and mental healing, Mary, with other women, accompanied Jesus and the disciples and contributed to their support. Mary was one of those who stood by the cross, attempting to comfort the Lord by her presence. After the Sabbath, she was at the tomb early to anoint His body. Upon discovering the empty tomb and informing the disciples, she stayed at the tomb in sorrow while Peter and John investigated quickly and then left.

When two angels appeared and asked Mary why she was weeping, her reply was tender: "Because they have taken away my Lord, and I do not know where they have laid Him" (John 20:13 NKJV).

Then the precious woman who loved *her* Lord with all her heart encountered the resurrected Christ. At first she thought He was the gardener. Then He spoke her name: "Mary." When she recognized His voice, her heart must have fairly burst with praise and adoration. Mary's fervent, single-hearted love was steadfast and set forever upon her Lord. For that she has been highly honored.

To love the Lord with the fervent devotion that Mary Magdalene lavished upon Jesus has everything to do with how we set the direction of our hearts. As Mary Duncan observes, "It is not because of *perfect* love that God will deliver. It is to the will to love and serve— it is to the *setting* of the heart, that the promise is made—to the 'full purpose of heart' that is *set* to cleave unto the Lord."[3]

The Promise of Deliverance

When our love is set upon the Lord, He promises to deliver us. The life of the godly prophet Daniel testifies to this promise. His heart was so set upon God that when a law was passed forbidding prayer to anyone but the king, Daniel defied the law by continuing to pray to his God. Daniel's envious enemies saw to it that King Darius was informed, and Daniel was sent to the lions' den. Darius, distressed and anxious for Daniel, exclaimed to him, "May your God, whom you worship continually, rescue you" (Dan. 6:16 NLT). Very early the next morning Darius called out, "Daniel, servant of the living God! Was your God, whom you worship continually, able to rescue you from the lions?" (Dan. 6:20 NLT). Because Daniel loved and trusted God, the answer was a victorious "Yes!"

The Hebrew word for *deliver* means to "be rescued, liberated," but it can also mean "to equip for a fight, to strengthen."[4] There is a clear illustration of this second meaning in Abram's life. After Abram had marshaled his army and rescued Lot from capture by the kings of Mesopotamia, he was met by the king of Sodom and by Melchizedek, king of Salem. Melchizedek blessed him with these words: "And blessed be God Most High, who has delivered your enemies into your hand" (Gen. 14:20 NKJV).

Although Abram loved and trusted God, he didn't just wait around for supernatural deliverance from the Lord. He and his three hundred and eighteen servants attacked the kings in order to deliver Lot. The king of Salem acknowledged that God delivered victory, but He did so by equipping and strengthening Abram for the task.

God will deliver those whose hearts are set on Him, but it is deliverance in His way and for His purposes. My idea of deliverance is that I am immediately freed from any difficulty! But instant rescue is not always the Lord's way. Daniel was delivered, but he still had to spend a night in the lions' den. God delivered Abram's enemies into his hands, but Abram still had to fight.

God's deliverance is not limited to the physical realm. Often His deliverance is accomplished in our spirits. The apostle Peter, in his own strength, pledged his undying love for Jesus. But when he found himself in discomforting circumstances, he readily denied knowing Jesus. Afterward, Peter went out and wept bitterly.

That may look like failure to us, but God was using the failure in a process of deliverance. Peter, who did love the Lord, needed to be freed from his self-reliance. His human confidence was rooted in pride in his own ability to serve. A humble and contrite Peter knew that apart from the Lord, he could do nothing. In his contrition, he was refreshed, revived, and delivered.

KNOWING THE NAME OF GOD

Another promise from your Father appears in Psalm 91:14. When you know His name, you will be set on high with Him.

On numerous occasions women have come up to me and asked, "Do you remember me?" Most of the time I remember the face, but I cannot recall the name. How special they would feel if I could immediately say, "Oh, yes, of course, you're Mary!"

Names are very important to God. He calls you by name. Your name is written on the palms of His hands and in the Book of Life. His name is most significant of all, and He is pleased when you know it.

Knowing God's name means that we understand His true character. It does not mean that we have acquired a collection of intellectual facts about God. This knowledge is highly personal: it springs from a loving intimacy with Him. It means believing and loving Jesus Christ, His living Word. Faith and trust are the pillars of this relationship.

The Scriptures use special names for God that portray His attributes. We know that one of His names is *holy*. His name is excellent, worthy of receiving glory and being exalted. It is to be called upon, feared, hallowed, and blessed. It provides safety: "The name of the LORD is a strong tower; the righteous run to it and are safe" (Prov. 18:10 NKJV).

God's name is *Father*. When you know your Father intimately, He will set you on high. God is the High and Lofty One who dwells in eternity. When you know Him, you become His child who is *in* but not *of* ("set above") the things of the world. Paul proclaimed, "Since you have been raised to new life with Christ, set your sights on the realities of heaven, where Christ sits at God's right hand in the place of honor and power. Let heaven fill your thoughts. Do not think only about things down here on earth" (Col. 3:1–2 NLT).

If you are set on high, you are up close to your Father. This closeness impels you to seek His kingdom and His righteousness above all things. Your reward for setting your heart to know your Father is His deliverance from all that can truly harm you: this is security beyond measure, and it results in intimacy with Him.

The Lord's Prayer began with *Abba*, as Jesus told his disciples how to speak to God. He gave them the right to use this term of intimacy and familiarity—the intimacy of divine *Daddy*ness with Almighty God, the Creator of the heavens and earth!

In that moment, the entire foundation of our relationship with God was changed: Jesus declared that God was forevermore to be our *daddy*!

You may approach the Father closely and intimately now, he said—yourselves!

The God of fire and thunder, the God upon whom no man can look, the Holy and Almighty, the Sovereign of Sinai, the great and terrible has now also become your *Daddy . . . Abba.*

—Michael Phillips[5]

For Reflection

Why do you think Psalm 91:14 so closely connects being delivered by God with knowing His name?

Tell God in prayer how you desire to set your heart on Him, trusting in His protection and deliverance.

KEY THOUGHT FOR DEEPER INTIMACY: *The Father holds me very close when I set my heart upon knowing and loving Him above all else.*

The Father speaks *(what is He saying to you?)*:

The child responds *(what are you saying to Him?)*:

PART TWO

The Father's Listening Ear

THE FATHER AND THE CHILD

The child spoke:

Father, how can You hear my voice among all who call upon You?

My child, I know your name; I know the number of hairs on your head; I know your own special voice.

Sometimes it's hard for me to know how to talk to You.

Although I am always ready to listen, you need not be anxious about what to say. Coming into My presence is what is most important.

Sometimes I don't sense Your presence. I feel that I have not heard from You.

You must learn to rely on the truth, not on your feelings. You are My beloved child. My Word declares My love to you. My Spirit dwelling within you can reassure you.

Thank You for listening to me when I cry out to You.

I am your Father, who loves you deeply. It pleases Me to know that you are depending on Me for your direction, deliverance, and strength.

Why can't I remember that I should always come to You for help?

The more you hear My voice, the more you will remember to call upon Me.

O Father, Your love, patience, and involvement in my life are humbling.
All I want is to keep growing in my relationship with You.

And you will, Child, for I delight in hearing your voice and answering you.

8

He Hears
My Voice

I love the LORD, because He has heard
My voice and my supplications.
Because He has inclined His ear to me,
Therefore I will call upon Him as long as I live.

—*Psalm 116:1–2 NKJV*

Our oldest daughter is an audiologist. When an acquaintance learned of our daughter's vocation, he told us about how he had been unaware of his own steady decline in hearing until his family sat him down before Christmas to tell him about their gift to him that year. They had made an appointment for him with an audiologist so that he could be fitted for hearing aids. He hadn't realized it, but over time he had been speaking more and more loudly and was continually asking family members to repeat what they had just said. The family made it clear that if he chose not to go to the audiologist, they would choose to ignore his requests to "speak up" or repeat their last remark. These dear children wanted a father who could hear them!

There are few occasions more satisfying than having someone's listening ear. When a friend looks you in the eye and absorbs your every word, you feel singled out and accepted. I love to be listened to, but I don't always love to listen. I often find myself confessing my inattentiveness while conversing with friends. In the midst of our visit, my mind will wander, and then my friend will ask a question I can't answer. I would do well to remember this thought: "A good listener is not only popular everywhere, but after a while he knows something."[1] A good listener is indeed popular. The psalmist's testimony in 116:1–2 indicates that a good listener is loved.

Most scholars believe that David was the author of Psalm 116. No one could make the statement in these opening verses unless prayer was his daily experience. How could anyone make such certain declarations about the Lord's responses if he never prayed or if he prayed only sporadically? We know that throughout David's life, he regularly called out to God. His love was steadfast and his relationship so fixed on the Lord that he could speak with great credibility concerning God's listening ear.

The background circumstances for this psalm involve the writer's deliverance from death:

> Death had its hands around my throat;
>   the terrors of the grave overtook me . . .
> The LORD protects those of childlike faith;
>   I was facing death, and then he saved me. (116:3, 6 NLT)

Some translations use the word *Sheol* for "death." It represents the world of the dead, the grave, the pit, or hell. Apparently, some very serious illness or near fatal crisis had threatened the psalmist's life. Whatever his dire circumstances, they had compelled him to cry out to God for help.

Notice the psalmist's immediate response in the face of adversity: he called upon the Lord. What is your first impulse when you get bad news? Do you turn immediately to the Lord? If not, perhaps you might need greater confidence that you have His listening ear.

DEVELOPING CONFIDENCE THAT GOD HEARS US

Early in David's life, he learned of God's faithful protection during his years as a shepherd. When Goliath was taunting the army of Israel, David convinced King Saul that he was capable of defeating the giant: "The LORD who saved me from the claws of the lion and the bear will save me from this Philistine!" (1 Sam. 17:37 NLT).

David continued to see God's hand of deliverance through his struggles with Saul's vindictiveness and his many victorious battles against the enemies of Israel. In Psalm 86:13 (NKJV), David sang, "For great is Your mercy toward me, and You have delivered my soul from the depths of Sheol." Over and over again, David acknowledged God's grace and mercy in his life. No wonder he loved the Lord; he was a personal recipient of God's everlasting love. He knew firsthand the Father's concern and care for His children.

David built his confidence in God's listening ear through many life experiences. Psalm 116 offers thanks for a physical deliverance. The apostle Paul's prison experiences express the same love and gratitude for God's mercy in His protection of our souls. At Paul's preliminary hearing for his imprisonment in Rome, he was all alone. There was no one to stand with him and encourage his heart. "But the Lord stood with me and gave me strength," he testified, "that I might preach the Good News in all its fullness for all the Gentiles to hear. And he saved me from certain death. Yes, and the Lord will deliver me from every evil attack and will bring me safely to his heavenly Kingdom. To God be the glory forever and ever. Amen" (2 Tim. 4:17–18 NLT).

Paul echoed David's heartfelt belief in the Lord's unwavering commitment to hear and respond when we are in need. Paul experienced God's deliverance through being strengthened when he was abandoned. He was also delivered from immediate execution at the hands of the Roman emperor. Paul spoke confidently of the Lord's continued deliverance of him from every evil. Paul knew that his death was imminent, and he viewed it not as a victory for Rome but as a sign of God's ultimate liberation. Paul could wholeheartedly proclaim along with David, "I love the Lord because He has heard my voice and my supplications."

STAYING ON HEARING TERMS WITH GOD

To be confident that the Lord hears us, we must be sure that we are on hearing terms with Him. Isaiah 59:1–2 (NKJV) instructs us in this respect:

> Behold, the LORD'S hand is not shortened,
> That it cannot save;
> Nor His ear heavy,
> That it cannot hear.
> But your iniquities have separated you from your God;
> And your sins have hidden His face from you,
> So that He will not hear.

These verses say that God is not deaf, but our sins can cause such a separation that God does not hear us. These are sins that we don't acknowledge, sins that we don't want to let go of. When we harbor sin in our lives, our prayers become insincere. We no longer have God's listening ear because we are not on hearing terms with Him. If our prayer life seems dull, it's safe to say that the dullness is always on our side.

When Jesus taught us to pray, He instructed us to ask forgiveness of our sins daily. Psalm 139:23–24 (NLT) provides a good model:

> Search me, O God, and know my heart;
>   test me and know my thoughts.
> Point out anything in me that offends you,
>   and lead me along the path of everlasting life.

God's name is holy, and He delights in hearing the prayers of His contrite and humble children.

As I consider my life, I am deeply grateful for the Lord's desire to hear my voice. Even though I continually mumble and grumble, He listens faithfully. He doesn't say, "Oh, no, it's Cynthia again!" From His eternal habitation, He graciously inclines His ear and gives me His full, undivided attention.

The Lord never asks me to speak up or repeat myself. His ear is not dull! I am His child, and He is pleased when I come to pour out my heart. It grieves Him when I try to work out my problems in my own way or try to "fix" my circumstances or someone else's life without His help, direction, or permission. It pleases Him when I am content with the knowledge that He has heard my requests; it grieves Him when my voice grows demanding or dictatorial. It pleases Him when I trust His love and His guidance; it grieves Him when I try to short-circuit His divine plan for my life. Time and again I realize that the safest way for me is staying on hearing terms with God.

HE LISTENS AND ACTS FOR YOUR GOOD

Knowing that the Lord hears is an excellent reason for loving God, but it is not the only reason. Our confidence that God hears us also includes the knowledge that He cares for us and will deliver us for our good.

When someone really listens to you, you know that she truly cares for you and wants to help you—whether through her involvement in your circumstances or through strengthening your heart to persevere. When you share your concerns with someone who listens carefully, you are often implicitly asking for her guidance and counsel, but sometimes the simple act of sharing your struggles is enough to keep you going. You have shared your burden with another, and it is no longer quite so heavy.

As I cast my cares upon the Lord, many times His response to me is that He has heard, that He loves me, and that He will be with me. I may not know how He will act or what He will do specifically with the cares I bring before Him. But that is not the important issue. Rather, it is whether I will place my confidence in Him that He hears me and will act for my good. Can I trust Him? Is it enough to know that He has heard my voice?

David, Paul, and countless others proclaimed the faithfulness of the Lord in hearing their petitions. They knew that God hears us because He loves us. That prompted David to exclaim, "Because He has inclined His ear to me, / Therefore I will call *upon Him* as long as I live."

The Scriptures are wonderfully descriptive. I love the picture of the Lord *inclining* His ear. Have you ever conversed with someone who pushed his chair back away from you and folded his arms? Body language communicates how much someone wants to be involved with you or distanced from you. Our Father *inclines* His ear to you. He is open to you; He has a preference for you; He is attracted to you; He is interested in you. He says, "Oh, here comes My beloved child. I want to listen to her voice!" This *inclining* inspired David to promise that he would continue to call upon the Lord all his life.

To continue calling upon the Lord means that, in a sense, I never stop conversing with Him. Isn't that what the Father wants, to hold us close so that we can have unbroken communion with Him? As I hold His hand throughout the day, it is natural that I turn to Him and verbalize not only my concerns, but also my love and praise. I love the Lord because He hears my voice. I will call upon Him all my life, confident with Paul that the Lord will act for my good until He brings me "safely to his heavenly Kingdom."

Don't be fooled. Because I can talk with God so easily and simply today doesn't mean that it was always so. The price you have to pay is willingness to control your mind and thoughts, willingness to submit to God's discipline, willingness to keep at it even when you seem to make little progress . . . But after a while—and I don't mean years and years, but months or even weeks, if you really mean business you will find that what was hard effort has become a great joy. Because you love God, and know he loves you, the strain quickly goes out of the relationship, and his love excites you—that's the only word that really describes it—excites you with a longing to be with him and talk with him.

—Brother Lawrence[2]

For Reflection

Reflect on Psalm 116:1–2. Why do you think the psalmist responded with love to the knowledge that God was listening to him?

Share with your Father how you desire to continually call upon Him.

KEY THOUGHT FOR DEEPER INTIMACY: *My Father bends His ear and draws closer to me when I continually call upon Him.*

The Father speaks *(what is He saying to you?)*:

The child responds *(what are you saying to Him?)*:

9

He Answers Me

In the day when I cried out, You answered me,
And made me bold with strength in my soul.

—*Psalm 138:3* NKJV

*H*ave you ever left a message for your doctor to call you and then waited all day for his reply? You can't leave the house because you might miss him, and every time the phone rings, you're disappointed when it's not him. When the doctor does call, it's such a relief to get an answer or some advice from him.

With today's automated technology, speaking to a real person is a rarity! No matter what our needs, it can be frustratingly difficult to get a response to our request. We live in a quick-fix society, but we don't always have quick access to those who can give us the answers we need.

Easy access and a listening ear are blessings offered by the Father to His obedient child. He is always on call. David knew that well, and he took full advantage of his loving relationship with the Lord in calling upon Him continually. In Psalm 138:3, he expressed his gratitude for the Lord's answer.

ALL YOU HAVE TO DO IS CALL

David had no trouble crying out to the Lord. He never hesitated; he easily and confidently lifted his voice to the One he knew could help. He poured out his heart; he wept; he pleaded for the Lord's intervention. Listen to this vivid cry:

> My enemy has chased me.
>> He has knocked me to the ground.
>> He forces me to live in darkness like those in the grave.
> I am losing all hope;
>> I am paralyzed with fear. (Ps. 143:3–4 NLT)

There was no soft-pedaling; David forthrightly and honestly cast his burden upon the Lord. He cried because he knew God heard, cared, and answered.

I struggle with feeling I have to be strong when I speak with the Lord. I think I'm supposed to exhibit all the fruit of the Spirit even when I'm in great distress. I think I should be joyful, patient, kind toward any enemy that might assail me. I want to show the Lord what a "big girl" I am. I want to be strong in my own strength!

In truth, I am the Father's imperfect child who will always be in the process of growing. So what should I do with these feelings of desperation, this sense of a crushed spirit? Our Father wants us, His children, to share freely our whole hearts with Him. My relief always lies in being honest with Him.

David is a wonderful role model for how to cast your burden upon the Lord and find relief for your soul. How refreshing it is to read his prayers. He truly lifted up his soul to his Father: "God, here is what's going on, and this is how I feel. I'm losing all hope, and I'm paralyzed with fear. I need You!" David easily became the child seeking refuge and solace from his Father. He admitted his inability to save himself, his total dependence on God. His intimate knowledge of God enabled him to say, "I will call on the LORD, who is worthy of praise, for he saves me from my enemies" (Ps. 18:3 NLT). David did not try to do for himself what he knew only God could do. What David did well was cry. What God did well was answer—and He still does!

WHEN AND HOW HE ANSWERS

In Psalm 138:3, David praised the Lord for answering on the day he cried. God heard and responded immediately. Eliezer, Abraham's servant, could also praise God for an instant answer to prayer. Abraham had commissioned Eliezer to secure a bride for Isaac from Abraham's family in Mesopotamia. As Eliezer entered the city of Nahor, he prayed that he would know the young woman who was to be Isaac's bride by her positive response to his request for water and her gracious offer to water his camels as well.

The Scriptures tell us exactly what happened when Eliezer offered up his prayer: "And it happened, before he had finished speaking, that behold, Rebekah, who was born to Bethuel, son of Milcah, the wife of Nahor, Abraham's brother, came out with her pitcher on her shoulder" (Gen. 24:15 NKJV). Rebekah gave water to Eliezer for him and for his camels. When he found out that she was Abraham's relation, he bowed his head and worshiped the Lord. *In the day when I cried out, You answered me!* God often answers prayers before we have even finished speaking.

We have already considered the Lord's blessing on Solomon when he requested wisdom to lead the nation. God answered the newly crowned king by giving him what he asked for (wisdom), but He also gave Solomon more than he asked for (riches and honor). God often will grant our request and then give superabundantly more than we asked.

Sometimes God delays His answer or responds differently from what we had hoped because we ask out of our own narrow concerns, and He has something bigger and better in mind.

When Lazarus, the brother of Martha and Mary, fell ill, the sisters sent for Jesus, saying, "Lord, behold, he whom You love is sick" (John 11:3 NKJV). Yet John indicated that because Jesus loved the three, He waited two days before traveling to Bethany. By the time Jesus arrived, Lazarus had been dead four days.

The answer from Jesus to their call of distress was perplexing to

Martha and Mary. They knew the Lord loved them, and they knew He could heal. But Jesus came too late! Why had He waited so long? A commentator on this passage provides a helpful clue: "It is true that there is sometimes delay in the answer to our prayer; but, in that case, delay is the answer."[1]

Martha and Mary wanted Jesus to heal Lazarus, but Jesus wanted to do more. He wanted to confirm in their hearts that He was the Messiah. He wanted to deepen their trust. He wanted to make the strongest possible impression on the unbelieving Jews at the tomb. He wanted to bring glory to God.

How focused we can become on our own little world, and how easily we grow impatient. We forget that our Father has bigger plans for us. They have to do with His kingdom. Sometimes, this means He will not answer on the day that we cry. But He will always answer.

Sometimes the *how* of God's answer is more important than the *when*. Paul discovered that when he pleaded with the Lord to remove a thorn in his flesh. Apparently, the Lord answered quickly, for Paul recounted, "Each time he said, 'My gracious favor is all you need. My power works best in your weakness'" (2 Cor. 12:9 NLT). In that circumstance, Paul prayed and the Lord answered, but His answer was no.

It is hard to receive no for an answer. Paul asked three times. Yet it is an answer, and when it comes, we must accept it with trust that it is for our benefit. The thorn was for Paul's good, to keep him from exalting himself and to ensure that he remained dependent on God. Once Paul accepted God's answer, he changed his original request: "So now I am glad to boast about my weaknesses, so that the power of Christ may work through me. Since I know it is all for Christ's good, I am quite content . . . For when I am weak, then I am strong" (2 Cor. 12:9–10 NLT).

God's answer to the apostle's prayer was His strength in place of Paul's weakness. This response echoes David's experience, as he recounted it in Psalm 138:3 (NKJV): "You answered me, and made me bold with strength in my soul." When you cry out to God to deliver you from trouble, can you accept that His answer will sometimes take the form of His strength for you in the midst of the difficulties?

Consider the agony Jesus endured as He prayed in the Garden of Gethsemane. He was overwhelmed by the prospect of being separated from His Father, a terrible condition He had never experienced. His sweat became like drops of blood because He, who knew no sin, was to become sin for us. Luke recorded how Jesus cried out to His Father: "Father, if it is Your will, take this cup away from Me; nevertheless not My will, but Yours, be done" (Luke 22:42 NKJV).

Here is a specific request made to the Father by His beloved Son. How did the Father respond? The answer was no. But that was not all of the answer. The verse following Jesus' prayer tells us, "Then an angel appeared to Him from heaven, strengthening Him." *In the day when I cried out, You answered me, and made me bold with strength in my soul.*

Psalm 116, which we looked at in the previous chapter as testimony that God hears us, is a Passover psalm. It is most likely the psalm Jesus recited with His disciples the night He was arrested. Remember? "I love the LORD, because He has heard my voice and my supplications."

Your Father hears you. He inclines His ear to you. He listens to your pleas. He answers as your Father should—for your good and His glory. But no matter what form the answer takes, when He gives it, He always holds you close to strengthen and protect you. Sometimes, this is the best answer of all.

We are accustomed to say that a man is not utterly lost until he has *lost heart.* But if God supplies inward strength, we never shall lose heart, and so never shall be lost. God is prepared ever to make a man's soul very rich. He may be very full of troubles; God can make his soul quiet and calm with Divine peace; God can comfort him with the support of "the everlasting arms." Outwardly a man may be tossed about, worn, wearied, wounded, almost broken; yet inwardly he may be kept in perfect peace; he may be "strong in the Lord, and in the power of his might."

—R. Tuck[2]

For Reflection

Consider David's affirmation in Psalm 138:3. Why would he refer to the strengthening of his soul as an answer to his prayer?

Offer your gratitude to God for His wisdom in when and how He answers you.

KEY THOUGHT FOR DEEPER INTIMACY: *When I cry to my Father, He hears and strengthens me and holds me close.*

The Father speaks *(what is He saying to you?)*:

The child responds *(what are you saying to Him?)*:

10

He Invites Me to
Be Alone with Him

But when you pray, go into your most private room, and closing the door, pray to your Father Who is in secret; and your
Father Who sees in secret will reward you *in the open*.

—*Matthew 6:6* AMPLIFIED

How would you like to be called a "phony," an "impostor," a
"deceiver," and a "hypocrite"? How would you like it if you were
being called these names by the Lord Himself? If you had been a
Pharisee living at the time of Jesus' public ministry, that might well
have been your experience. You would likely have heard Jesus'
rebuke of your legalistic pursuit of God.

The Pharisees were a religious society of Judaism. They became
the institutional leaders who formalized the law of the Jewish
scribes. The word *Pharisees* means "the separated ones." Qualifica-
tions for membership included a pledge to live in strict adherence
to the Law and to practice ceremonial purity.

The Pharisees' strict adherence to their code soon fostered in
them a sense of superiority and pride. They separated themselves
from anyone who did not live as they did. As they practiced the
Law and its traditions, their religion defined itself around external
behavior. Performance, or *doing* the commandments, became more
important than a sincere heart and the motivation to please God.

An outward show of their piety resulted in a legalistic approach to worship.

Consequently, when Jesus appeared, the Pharisees were extremely threatened by His message of unconditional love and salvation by grace. They frequently challenged and opposed the Lord, and they ultimately orchestrated His death. Jesus usually referred to them as "hypocrites," reproving them for their ostentation, lovelessness, and self-righteousness.

In contrast to the practices of the Pharisees, the Lord taught His disciples how to give, to pray, and to fast. When He began teaching on prayer, He started by saying, "When you pray you must not be like the hypocrites, for they love to pray standing in the synagogues and on the corners of the streets, that they may be seen by people. Truly, I tell you, they have their reward—in full already" (Matt. 6:5 AMPLIFIED). How tragic to be used as a negative example, especially in the appropriate way to pray!

Until Jesus came, however, there really were no other religious role models. The Pharisees were the leaders and teachers. In the "How to Pray Effectively as a Pharisee" course, you were taught to stand in the most public places so that others could see your piety and reward you with their praise and honor. The Pharisees prayed to be heard by people, not by God.

All Jesus could say in response to the Pharisees' prayer life was, "Don't do it the way they do—do the opposite! Pray privately. Prayer is communion, not a performance." Jesus does not say it is wrong to pray publicly, but He teaches that the rewards for praying in secret are far greater than those for praying in public.

THE TREASURE OF SECRET PRAYER

Jesus taught that if you wish to draw close to your Father in prayer, then go into your private room, your closet, any place you can be by yourself. Only when you are alone can you discover the treasure of speaking to your Father in secret. In private, you can be yourself, a child who converses with her Father. It is hard to be pretentious or artificial because no one else is there to watch; you need not maintain a particular posture or pray in a certain prescribed way. Praying in secret allows you to be honest, to cry, to talk out loud, and to listen.

Perhaps you are asking, "Do *private* rooms really exist? There are none in my home!" Some rooms are private only at certain times—mostly early in the morning or late at night. Hudson Taylor, missionary to China, often had his time of communion at 2:00 A.M. He would retire at a reasonable hour, wake at 2:00, and after a time of Scripture reading and prayer, continue his sleep until morning.

Sometimes the "closet" can be outside. Mark recorded that Jesus "got up and went out to a deserted place, and there He prayed" (1:35 AMPLIFIED). Jesus didn't even have a place to lay His head, and everywhere He went He was surrounded by people. Yet prayer was such a necessity for Him that He found gardens, hillsides, any deserted places to be with His Father.

My closet is often the neighborhood when I am taking a walk—just the Lord and me. There are no interruptions and very few distractions. If your life is one continual demand after another, then you know that your private room can be any place you choose to quiet your heart and enter the presence of the Lord. Susanna Wesley, who had nineteen children, withdrew into her closet by putting her apron over her head!

In reality, our prayer closet is in our hearts. John Chrysostom counseled, "No one should give the answer that it is impossible for a man occupied with worldly cares to pray always. You can set up an altar to God in your mind by means of prayer. And so it is fitting to pray at your trade, on a journey, standing at a counter or sitting at your handicraft."[1] A particular place is not as essential as a pure heart and the desire to be alone with God, wherever that place might be.

THE IMPORTANCE OF CLOSING THE DOOR

After you have chosen to spend time in your prayer closet, it is important to "close the door." For me, closing the door is a conscious choice to lay aside any temporal concerns that would hinder my concentration during prayer. Often I have purposed to pray, but as I begin, my mind suddenly fills with all my pressing responsibilities. This means I did not shut the door on the world.

Some of the distractions are issues that will need my attention. I keep a piece of paper with me and write them down so I won't forget about them later. This exercise helps me either to pray about my list or to put it out of my mind for a while.

Another help in drawing near to God and away from the world is to read Scripture. The best way to begin prayer is to let the Lord speak first. The whole intent of secret prayer is to be in the presence of the Lord, to speak with Him as a child would share with someone she dearly loved and trusted.

To be alone with someone I love is a precious gift. A dear friend and mentor flew to Tucson to spend a few days with me. I was thrilled that she came expressly to see me—alone! I didn't have to share her with anyone; it was just the two of us. She came because she loved me. Whenever she is free to visit, I will make any arrangements to be with her. My time with her will always be a priority.

Even more, this is the way I feel about the Lord. He proclaims His love for me, He inclines His ear to hear my voice, and He is available any time of the day or night. Why wouldn't I respond gladly to His desire to spend secret time together?

What a privilege and blessing to commune with the Father, who not only hears, but also sees:

> The LORD looks down from heaven
>> and sees the whole human race.
> From his throne he observes
>> all who live on the earth.
> He made their hearts,
>> so he understands everything they do. (Ps. 33:13–15 NLT)

Job's friend Elihu observed: "For His eyes are on the ways of man, and He sees all his steps" (Job 34:21 NKJV).

THE JOY OF EYE CONTACT WITH GOD

God not only inclines His ear to us, but He also looks us in the eye. We are not praying to "Someone up there" who is so high above us that He cannot see or hear. Through the power of His Holy Spirit, He sees, hears, and is very present in our hearts.

What does God see? He sees our hearts. He sees the vanity of the hypocrite or the desire of His child who wants to sit at His feet. Jesus tells us that He sees our needs: "Your Father knows what you need before you ask Him" (Matt. 6:8 AMPLIFIED). The knowledge that God is ever-present and all-knowing encourages me to flee to Him often. He knows everything anyway, so why not talk it all over with Him and leave my closet with His guidance and peace?

How it pleases our Father when we take time to enter His presence, desiring secret communion with Him. He has provided everything necessary for our intimacy with Him. He waits for us to go into a private room, shut the door, and lift up our hearts to Him.

When we come to God secretly, He rewards us openly. Sometimes the reward is renewed strength in the spirit. Sometimes it includes a direct answer to prayer. Often it is the assurance of His presence and guidance. What a great reward it is just to be met by the Lord, knowing that He cares and that we are worthy to be loved and listened to. This is an honor in itself.

The Pharisees were rewarded publicly by the praise of men in the synagogue. Our ultimate reward will be granted before all the world on that great day when every knee shall bow and every tongue confess that Jesus Christ is Lord. What a joy to be among those who deepened their intimacy with the Father through rich times of secret prayer.

> It is no use to ask what those who love God do with Him. There is no difficulty in spending our time with a friend we love; our heart is always ready to open to Him; we do not

study what we shall say to Him, but it comes forth without premeditation; we can keep nothing back—even if we have nothing special to say, we like to be with Him.

—François Fenelon[2]

For Reflection

Consider Jesus' teaching in Matthew 6:6. Why do you think God rewards secret prayer?

Take time this day to draw close to your Father in secret prayer.

KEY THOUGHT FOR DEEPER INTIMACY: *Every time I meet secretly with the Father, I deepen my intimacy with Him.*

The Father speaks *(what is He saying to you?)*:

The child responds *(what are you saying to Him?)*:

11

He Gives Me Words to Pray

Our Father in heaven,
  may your name be honored.
May your Kingdom come soon.
May your will be done here on earth,
  just as it is in heaven.
Give us our food for today,
and forgive us our sins,
  just as we have forgiven those who have sinned against us.
And don't let us yield to temptation,
  but deliver us from the evil one.

—*Matthew 6:9–13* NLT

I have repeated the Lord's Prayer innumerable times. Before some of the newer translations were published, I would often be confused by saying "debts" when everyone else said "trespasses" and saying "trespasses" when everyone else said "debts." I always seemed to be more concerned about saying the words correctly than personally praying these thoughts to God.

We miss out on rich times with the Lord if we treat this prayer only as a traditional part of church services and leave it there. The Lord gave us this prayer, and it is a guide to speaking intimately with our Father.

Jesus followed His teaching on praying in private with this beautiful model of prayer. It came upon the heels of His warning against praying as the heathen did, who mumbled thoughtless words in futile repetitions. When Elijah challenged the priests of Baal to invoke their god's power to send fire and consume a sacrifice, the priests cried incessantly all morning, "O Baal, hear us!" (1 Kings 18:26 NKJV). The repetitions were certainly in vain, for Baal never answered.

The Lord used the heathen and the hypocrites as examples of how not to pray: don't think you have prayed just because you chanted certain words over and over again; and don't publicize your prayer life so that everyone can see how pious you are. And you don't have to go into a lot of detail because your Father knows the things you need before you ask.

The prayer Jesus taught us is simple and brief because He wanted to assure His disciples that long, elaborate explanations were not necessary with God.

But in this manner pray . . . Jesus gives us a form or model of prayer, which includes the essential elements of personal prayer. I am thankful to have a pattern of how to pray so I know that I am praying as I should. Also, I feel that if I pray these main petitions, then I have covered the necessary principles in prayer. My words may vary greatly each time I pray through this outline, but at least I am praying in the manner taught by the Lord.

ENTERING INTO HIS PRESENCE

Our Father. It is significant that the invocation begins the prayer personally. We don't say, "To the almighty, high and lofty, majestic, most holy God of the universe." It is simply *our Father.* We verbalize our intimate love for Him when we say, *Abba, Father,* declaring our dependence, our trust, and our identity as His children.

In heaven. Our Father inhabits eternity and dwells in a high and holy place. He is not limited by space or time. He knows all and sees all. He is sovereign. Although He is our Father whom we love intimately, we are to approach Him with awe.

May your name be honored. To be honored means to be revered, consecrated, hallowed. God's name is His nature. When we pray for His name to be highly respected, we ask that it be held sacred first in our hearts and then in the hearts of all men. "Sanctify the Lord God in your hearts," Peter wrote (1 Peter 3:15 NKJV). His name is holy, and we hallow it or sanctify it by walking in holiness.

May your Kingdom come soon. Asking for His kingdom to come is not just praying for the Lord's appearance and reign, but it is also committing ourselves to be a part of expanding His kingdom here on earth. I have heard this petition referred to as a missionary prayer: we are commissioned to share His good news so that many will become citizens of the kingdom of God. Since we don't know when His kingdom will come in all its fullness, this part of the prayer requires a long-term view. How I pray for this petition! I sympathize with the elderly gentleman who, when asked, "Do you see any signs of the Lord's coming soon?" answered, "No, but I see signs of my going soon!"

May your will be done here on earth, just as it is in heaven. In praying this petition, we are asking first that God's will be done in us. We cannot pray for God's purposes to be accomplished here on earth if we are not willing to yield to His will in our own lives. J. Oswald Sanders observed, "True prayer is not asking God for what *we* want, but for what *He* wants . . . Enable us to obey Thy revealed will as fully and as joyously as it is done by the angels in heaven."[1]

The first half of this pattern of prayer is focused on worship and adoration of God and the establishment of His kingdom. One of the ways I like to begin to pray is to read certain psalms that praise God and give expression to my wonder over His greatness and majesty. Certain hymns and spiritual songs help me to "shut the door" and come before His throne with a humble and contrite spirit.

The manner in which we are to pray is to worship and be concerned about the things of God as our first priority. Prayer for ourselves is secondary. We seek *first* His kingdom and His righteousness—then we can bring our needs to Him.

INTERCESSION FOR OURSELVES AND OTHERS

Our prayers do not provide information for God. Jesus teaches that He already knows our needs. Then why should we pray? Because the major part of prayer is praise, worship, submission, and commitment to seek the things above. When we pray as humble and contrite children, we realize our dependence and sense our need for our Father's provision in all areas of life. In verbalizing our needs, we allow God to be our Father—to provide, to comfort, to forgive, to guide, to bless. We are no longer striving and anxious; we are children who trust our Father.

Give us our food for today. God has a good track record in providing food daily. The Israelites could testify to God's faithfulness in supplying manna during their wilderness wanderings. God wants us to know that He is our provider. This is the only request in the Lord's Prayer concerning our bodies—food for the day.

And forgive us our sins. These are offenses against God. They are the thoughts and behaviors that violate the commands and instructions found in His Word. Sin separates us from God. When we ask for forgiveness, we seek the cleansing of our own hearts and the restoration of communion.

One of my prayers is, "Please let me know when I sin, and help me repent." I can think of nothing worse than sinning against someone and not knowing it. The Holy Spirit convicts us of sin, and my prayer is that I will always respond righteously to the sin pointed out in my life by asking forgiveness. David's cry for forgiveness can be ours:

> Have mercy upon me, O God,
> According to Your lovingkindness;
> According to the multitude of Your tender mercies,

Blot out my transgressions.

Wash me thoroughly from my iniquity,

And cleanse me from my sin. (Ps. 51:1–2 NKJV)

Just as we have forgiven those who have sinned against us. As we have received God's gracious forgiveness, so we must extend grace to those who have wronged us. Forgiving others is of extreme importance, so much so that at the conclusion of this prayer, Jesus adds that if we refuse to forgive others, neither will our Father forgive us (Matt. 6:15). Lawrence Richards explains, "It isn't that God will not forgive the unforgiving. It is simply that the unforgiving lack the humble attitude that both permits them to accept forgiveness and frees them to extend forgiveness."[2] If we are resentful and unforgiving, we are not free to receive God's grace and mercy. Forgiving others is for our benefit.

And don't let us yield to temptation, but deliver us from the evil one. The Scriptures tell us that our hearts are deceitful above all things and desperately wicked (Jer. 17:9). Because we cannot trust ourselves, this petition asks God to intervene in our lives and keep us from temptation and the evil one. We are giving God permission to exert His power on our behalf. My prayer is, "Lord, don't let me have my own way. Protect me from myself as well as the evil one! If I am headed in the wrong direction, please stop me." We have God's promise that when our love is set upon Him, He will deliver us.

This prayer is remarkably short, but it is conclusive. It stands in stark contrast to the prayers of the hypocrites and heathen. Their prayers are unnecessarily lengthened by vain repetitions; the Lord's Prayer is gloriously succinct. Its pattern is first to worship, then to ask—for daily bread, daily forgiveness, and daily deliverance. I am to ask not only for myself, but also for others. This is a wonderful intercessory prayer.

With the Holy Spirit helping you to pray and the Lord's Prayer as a guide, you now know how to begin your secret time with God. This is one of the best ways to deepen your intimacy with your Father.

Lord Jesus! Reveal to us the Father. Let His name, His infinite Father-love, the love with which He loved Thee, according to Thy prayer, be in us. Then shall we say aright, "Our Father!" Then shall we apprehend Thy teaching, and the first spontaneous breathing of our heart will be: "Our Father, Thy Name, Thy Kingdom, Thy Will" and we shall bring our needs and our sins and our temptations to Him in the confidence that the love of such a Father cares for all.

—Andrew Murray[3]

For Reflection

How can the prayer Jesus teaches in Matthew 6:9–13 cultivate deeper intimacy with the Lord?

Draw close to your heavenly Father by praying the Lord's Prayer.

KEY THOUGHT FOR DEEPER INTIMACY: *The more often I pray as Jesus taught, the more dependent I become upon my Father.*

The Father speaks *(what is He saying to you?):*

The child responds *(what are you saying to Him?):*

12

He Teaches Me
How to Spend My Days

So teach us to number our days,
That we may gain a heart of wisdom.

—*Psalm 90:12* NKJV

As I approached my fortieth birthday, I thought, *My life is half over!* At that time I had been married nineteen years. Our children were able to walk, dress themselves, and cut their own food. I was very content with my family, home, church, and friends. I did not mind getting older; in fact, I considered it a high privilege. I simply found it hard to fathom that I had already lived forty years. *Forty years is a long time. When did all these years accumulate?* I wondered. Had it really taken forty years to graduate from high school and college, marry, cook, clean, and care for our family of six? It seemed more like twenty-five.

If the first forty had sailed by, I knew that the last half of my life would probably pass even more quickly. Therefore I breathed this prayer: "Father, I don't know how many years I have left, but I want You to know that whatever time remains, I want to spend it in the center of Your will. I don't want to waste any time; I don't want to come to the end of my life with regrets. I want to be Your obedient child. I want to bring You glory." In this prayer, I did not have any preconceived ideas about what my life should look like. I just wanted to be sure that I was fully seeking His kingdom.

Neither was I looking for any change in my life. More than anything, I wanted to fulfill the Lord's purpose for me. I was giving Him full permission to mold me and use me.

That was my way of praying, "Teach me to number my days, that I may present to You a heart of wisdom." That was my cry for deeper intimacy.

COUNTING THE DAYS

Moses was the author of Psalm 90, a song most likely written toward the end of Israel's wanderings in the wilderness. Moses had led the people for almost forty years. The generation who had rejected God's leading into the promised land was dying, and Moses knew that his own death was imminent. In the midst of the chastisement, Moses penned this God-breathed psalm.

Moses began the prayer by declaring that God had always been their home, their refuge. That was in great contrast to the homelessness of Israel in the wilderness. He wrote that God is timeless, without beginning or end, contrasting the eternity of God with the temporality of man. Human life is like grass that springs up in the morning and by evening is dry and withered.

Then Moses turned to how Israel experienced God's anger at their sin, spending their brief lives in sorrow and ending them with a sigh. "Who can comprehend the power of your anger?" he wondered. "Your wrath is as awesome as the fear you deserve" (Ps. 90:11 NLT). Moses' question proposes that if God's anger against sin is rightly understood, then the fear and reverence due God will keep man from offending Him.

This is the context in which Moses pleaded, "Teach us to make the most of our time, so that we may grow in wisdom" (Ps. 90:12 NLT). *Since our lives are sinful, since our lives are brief, teach us, Lord, for You are the only One who is holy and everlasting.* It is a heartfelt prayer for discernment in how to live a fleeting life, an ancient prayer for anyone who desires to spend her days close to her Father.

We have already seen how God wants to teach us for our own

good and lead us in the way we should go (Isa. 48:17). How it must please Him to hear His child pray, "Teach me—I am listening, I am aware of my frailty, and I want only to live according to Your will." I recently asked the Lord to teach me by praying, "How can I simplify my life so that I have adequate time to sit at Your feet and accomplish in an orderly way my priorities and commitments? Teach me, O Lord, how to number my days."

One answer to my prayer was to stop producing a monthly devotional newsletter I had written for seventeen years. "Oh, no, Lord, You don't understand! This is Your word, and it is good to always present Your truth to others."

Cynthia, you asked how you could simplify your life, and this is My reply. Do you really want Me to teach you how to number your days?

To make the most of my days, I find that I need to keep Oswald Chambers's wise words in mind:

> In seeking the Best we soon find that our enemy is our good things, not our bad. The things that keep us back from God's best are not sin and imperfection, but the things that are right and good and noble from the natural standpoint. To discern that the natural virtues antagonize surrender to God is to bring our soul at once into the center of our greatest battlefield. Very few of us debate with the sordid and the wrong, but we do debate with the good.[1]

MAKING THE DAYS COUNT

"Teach me to number my days." What is necessary to make this request of the Lord and then apply His wisdom in how we spend our days?

First, we should ask of ourselves, Am I teachable? In asking to be taught to number our days, we're also asking God to lead us specifically in how to live our lives daily. And second, we need to be honest with ourselves in asking, Will I obey the Lord? Once we have learned to count our days, are we ready to make the days count?

It is interesting that Moses said "days." He didn't say, "Teach us to number our years." The image of days helps us to understand the brevity of life. We need to be concerned about each day, one at a time. Jesus told us to let go of worry about tomorrow: "Today's trouble is enough for today" (Matt. 6:34 NLT). We cannot presume on future days. We must live fully for the Lord the day we have now. All of us have known friends whose loved ones left home in the morning and, due to a heart attack, car wreck, or stroke, never came back. Life is uncertain. Therefore, O Lord, teach us how to make this day count for You.

In this perspective, each day becomes precious. Each day is a life in itself. My day may seem ordinary, filled with predictable routines, but it is a day to be lived with the Lord's wisdom and guidance. It is a day to be nourished by His Word and committed to His care and keeping.

With the Lord's Prayer as my example, I pray daily for His will, His provision, His forgiveness of me, my forgiveness of others, and my deliverance from evil. We gain wisdom—discernment, sound judgment, foresight—from praying daily. Each day enables us to live a life that pleases God and keeps us aware of the importance of living *today* for *eternity*.

A faithful servant is not caught off guard by the knowledge that life is fleeting. She is always ready to make the most of whatever the day may bring. She will never have to say to the Lord, "Oh, but I'm not prepared! I didn't realize You would be here so soon."

Years ago, in a small group, I was asked to write down what my priorities would be and what specific actions I would take if I knew I had only six months to live. What would I change? Whom would I spend time with? What would I read? What would my priorities be? After finishing the exercise and sharing our thoughts, our group heard this charge: *Now go and live by the guidelines you have written down.*

How would your life change if you knew you had only a few months to live? To begin answering this question, you can pray Moses' prayer for wisdom in numbering your days. It will remind you that life is transitory, and death is certain. Therefore, you should not be careless in how you live.

Jesus told a parable about a rich man who decided to build new and better barns because his old ones were overflowing. He was quite satisfied with his position in life, and he decided that for the rest of his life he would just take it easy. "But God said to him, 'You fool! You will die this very night. Then who will get it all?'" Jesus then explained, "Yes, a person is a fool to store up earthly wealth but not have a rich relationship with God" (Luke 12:16–21 NLT).

If you ask God to teach you to number your days, you will find that His answer involves developing a "rich relationship" with Him. All that really matters, ultimately, is the eternal. It is essential that you continually ask God to teach you how to spend your days. As you apply His teaching, you will become wise in discerning His will, you will become more richly related to Him, and you will look forward to an eternity of closeness with your Father.

> "Apply our hearts to wisdom." St. Austin says, "We can never do that, except we number every day as our last day."
>
> —William Seeker[2]

For Reflection

Consider Moses' request of God in Psalm 90:12. Why do you think he was concerned that the Israelites learn to number their days?

Express in prayer your wish to have a heart of wisdom.

KEY THOUGHT FOR DEEPER INTIMACY: *Asking my Father each day to teach me how to live wisely draws me into closer fellowship with Him.*

The Father speaks *(what is He saying to you?)*:

The child responds *(what are you saying to Him?)*:

13

He Cleanses My Heart

How can I know all the sins lurking in my heart?
Cleanse me from these hidden faults.
Keep me from deliberate sins!
Don't let them control me.
Then I will be free of guilt
and innocent of great sin.

—*Psalm 19:12–13* NLT

My friend paused as she was speaking to me. In the few seconds that she was silent, I interrupted her and finished her sentence. I do this often, out of impatience and a desire to demonstrate that I am listening. What sometimes happens, as it did in this instance, is that I do not finish my friend's sentence correctly. I wrongly presume that I know what the other person is going to say.

Sometimes I catch myself doing this but don't recognize that I really am disrupting the conversation. I can defend myself by rationalizing that I am only trying to help. But in reality, this is a hidden fault. *Lord, how can I know all the sins lurking in my heart? Cleanse me from these hidden faults.*

CLEANSE ME OF HIDDEN FAULTS

David began Psalm 19 by extolling the glory of the heavens. He went on to describe the beauty of God's Word, which revives the soul and brings joy to the heart. After the contemplation of God's vast heavens and the sufficiency of His Word, David then looked into his own heart. This is a natural progression. As we acknowledge God's revelation in creation and in His Word, we cannot help but examine our own souls in light of the glory and truth given to us.

Standing in awe of God and His Word can humble and convict His child. In another psalm, David cried,

> When I look at the night sky and see the work of your fingers—
> the moon and the stars you have set in place—
> what are mortals that you should think of us,
> mere humans that you should care for us? (Ps. 8:3–4 NLT)

Who are we, Lord, to be Your children—You, who are holy, majestic, and full of glory?

David continued to observe in Psalm 19 that God's Word is *perfect, right, clear, true,* and *pure.* The Word and its ministry pierced his heart to the point that he prayed, "Cleanse me from these hidden faults. Keep me from deliberate sins!" It is through the Word that we can come to a knowledge of sin. Paul wrote in Romans 7:7 (NLT), "It was the law that showed me my sin." And how blessed we are to have the Scriptures, for they play a vital role in maintaining our intimacy with our Father: "For the word of God is full of living power. It is sharper than the sharpest knife, cutting deep into our innermost thoughts and desires. It exposes us for what we really are" (Heb. 4:12 NLT). The Word humbles us and causes us to pray that even our secret offenses be cleansed, for sin estranges us from the Lord and robs us of intimacy.

David asked the question, "How can I know all the sins lurking in my heart?" Certainly, we can't. We know that the heart is deceitful and desperately wicked, so it is very easy to defend our faults.

The Pharisees are wonderful examples of self-deception. They thought they were being very righteous in dedicating their possessions to God. The practice enabled the Pharisees to use their finances for themselves, but not for others. If their parents needed help, they could "righteously" excuse themselves. Jesus denounced the practice specifically: "Thus you have made the commandment of God [Honor your father and mother] of no effect by your tradition. Hypocrites!" (Matt. 15:6–7 NKJV).

A Pharisee and a tax collector went to the temple to pray. The Pharisee proudly prayed, "I thank You, God, that I am not a sinner like everyone else, especially like that tax collector over there!" The tax collector prayed, "O God, be merciful to me, for I am a sinner." How the Pharisee needed to pray, "Lord, cleanse me from these hidden faults."

Hidden faults can be sins of ignorance, which we cannot discern. Others may see them, but we do not. As heinous as Paul's persecution of Christians was to the church, his sin was one of ignorance. He didn't know Christ. He really thought that what he was doing was right. He could not see his sin.

Some hidden offenses may not be as devastating or far-reaching as blatant and deliberate sins, but still they are hurtful. We may not be aware of habits of interrupting others, of speaking too bluntly, of speaking too much, but they are sins nonetheless:

> That such sins are sins, and need forgiveness, is plain from the fact that we blame ourselves on discovering them. "I was wrong; I did not see it: I meant to do right, but I see I was very wrong." We failed to see what a larger exercise of charity, or humility, or sympathy, or care and attention, would have enabled us to see. We judged too harshly, hastily, ignorantly. We were absorbed in some agreeable duty, and neglected a more urgent but uninteresting one.[1]

Since we cannot know our failings, we must ask God to cleanse our hearts. *Show me, Lord, cleanse me. Let me know how I wound others or how selfishly I serve myself.*

KEEP ME FROM DELIBERATE SINS

Not content just to be searched for hidden sins, David boldly asked God, "Keep me from deliberate sins! Don't let them control me." Another translation reads, "Keep back Your servant also from presumptuous sins" (NKJV). I like to say the word *presumptuous*. It sounds so haughty! And that is its meaning—"impertinent, insolent, brazen, willful, cocky, intentional." It describes sins we commit when we know better, but do them anyway.

David was kept from deliberate sin by the timely intervention of a wise woman. He was about to head off with his men and murder Nabal and his entire household for not offering them hospitality in acknowledgment of the protection that David and his men had extended to Nabal's servants out in the fields. Abigail, Nabal's wife, was informed of the impending disaster. She intercepted David and pleaded with him to spare their household and spare himself the weight on his conscience the bloodbath would surely incur. David gratefully replied to her entreaty, "Praise the LORD, the God of Israel, who has sent you to meet me today! Thank God for your good sense! Bless you for keeping me from murdering the man and carrying out vengeance with my own hands" (1 Sam. 25:32–33 NLT). Through Abigail, God kept David from presumptuous sin, and he was very thankful.

Unfortunately, David's life also provides a graphic example of his choice to commit deliberate sin. He knew the commandments, "Do not murder. Do not commit adultery." But he was presumptuous in carrying out his plan to commit adultery with Bathsheba and attempting to cover up by orchestrating Uriah's murder. When he was convicted of his great sin, he humbly repented and was graciously forgiven, but he suffered severe consequences for his presumption. In light of the experience, his prayer concerning deliberate sins was most personal and meaningful.

REMOVING THE BARRIER TO INTIMACY

The apostle John's teaching on sin reveals the characteristics of those who are intimate with the Father: "We know that those who have become part of God's family do not make a practice of sinning, for God's Son holds them securely, and the evil one cannot get his hands on them" (1 John 5:18 NLT). One way to confirm that you are God's child and part of His family is that you do not make a *practice* of sin. Your sin is not premeditated. I sin, but I do not *intend* to. I don't want to sin, but my impatience and insensitivity to others seem to rudely ignore my best intentions.

So we pray with David, "Keep me from deliberate sins! Don't let them control me." The Lord's Prayer echoes this plea: "Don't let us yield to temptation." This request gives God permission to restrain us. If this is our prayer, then we will be free from guilt and innocent of great sin.

We need to pray this prayer with fervor. It is too easy to slide into an affair. It is very tempting to lie. In the name of "vegging out," we watch programs or read books that might compromise our relationship with God. I constantly pray for God to show me my sin, asking Him to keep me from anything that would separate me from Him. Nothing this world has to offer is worth sacrificing my relationship with the Lord.

David fittingly ended Psalm 19 with the words,

> May the words of my mouth and the thoughts of my heart
>   be pleasing to you,
>   O LORD, my rock and my redeemer. (v. 14 NLT)

This is the perfect way to conclude the preceding requests. If your ardent desire is that your thoughts and words will please the Lord, then you will not find yourself plagued by hidden faults and presumptuous sins. If your conviction is that the Lord is your Rock and your Redeemer, then you know He holds you securely in His hand. There you will be blameless, innocent of great transgression and very close to the Father.

> And therefore, David, as one experienced in the deceitfulness of sin, doth thus digest and methodise his prayer: first against secret and lesser sins; and then against the more gross and notorious; as knowing the one proceeds and issues from the other: Lord, *cleanse me from my secret faults;* and this will be a most effectual means to preserve and *keep thy servant from presumptuous sins.*
>
> —Ezekiel Hopkins[2]

For Reflection

As you reflect on Psalm 19:12–13, consider why David so ardently prayed to be cleansed from hidden faults.

Lift up David's prayer for a clean heart to your Father.

KEY THOUGHT FOR DEEPER INTIMACY: *Asking God to cleanse my heart and keep me from sin enables Him to hold me very close.*

The Father speaks *(what is He saying to you?):*

The child responds *(what are you saying to Him?):*

14

He Draws Me to His Heart

One thing I have asked from the LORD,
   that I shall seek:
That I may dwell in the house of the LORD all the days of my life,
To behold the beauty of the LORD,
And to meditate in His temple.
For in the day of trouble He will conceal me in His tabernacle;
In the secret place of His tent He will hide me;
He will lift me up on a rock.

—*Psalm 27:4–5 NASB*

*S*everal couples had just finished a delicious meal. Our host asked each of us to answer this question: "If you were given the opportunity to do anything in the world you wanted, what would you choose to do?" We had varied, lighthearted answers: *Play unlimited golf, read, rest, travel, answer all my mail.* My answer was to sit in my comfortable chair, sip tea, and read some special books I was anxious to study and enjoy.

It was an entertaining exercise to think about really doing anything we wanted. Certainly, in the atmosphere of a dinner party, our answers were appropriate. But the question is a valid one we ought to consider seriously. What is the one thing to which I would like to devote my time and thoughts? What do I want to look forward to doing every day?

Had the psalmist David been at our table he would not have hesitated in his answer. He was confident in the one thing he wanted to do with his life; it was a settled matter. There was only one pursuit that mattered to him, and that was to dwell in the house of the Lord. He was a man after God's own heart.

CONTINUAL COMMUNION

David's overriding desire was to have constant communion with the Lord. As I think about his one request voiced in Psalm 27, I smile at what must have been God's great pleasure in hearing His servant's plea for intimacy. That was the mainspring and motivation of David's life. He had other desires, but the only important one was his relationship with God.

Above all David wanted closeness to his Father and deep spiritual insight. So his one petition was for spiritual welfare: "One thought has the mastery. One desire gives unity and concentration to all effort. One affection binds the heart and the life into a holy fellowship."[1]

As usual for David, he wrote the psalm while being pursued by his enemies. He declared that he didn't need to fear man because the Lord was the strength of his life. In fact, because of God's presence in his life, he saw his enemies stumble and fall. He was truly grateful for God's deliverance, and he yearned to center his whole life on worshiping the Lord. In the midst of his turmoil, David could have been craving many other things at that time in his life—permanent deliverance from enemies, some rest and peace—but he realized that there is only one essential: being in the presence of God.

David's decision to dwell with the Lord involved commitment, for he stated that he would *seek* to accomplish his desire. This is a good reminder for us of Jesus' call in Matthew 6:33, to seek first His kingdom. David was taking responsibility for seeing that his request was fulfilled. "I" have asked; "I" will seek to dwell.

James assured us that our longing for closeness will be fulfilled: "Draw near to God and He will draw near to you" (James 4:8 NKJV). If you desire intimacy, then you must seek it. God is always ready to be close to you. He waits only for you to come to Him. David's seeking was not sporadic, but constant and long term—"all the days of my life." He would seek the Lord not just when he needed help, but in all circumstances, all of his life. He would never cease pursuing his relationship with his God.

To dwell in the house of the Lord is to experience continual communion. His dwelling will become the place where you want to spend time, where you want to visit often, as His guest who experiences His protection and fellowship. You will approach His throne with great desire and receive blessing and encouragement with every minute in His presence.

This is what it means to abide in the Vine. To walk closely with your Father, you need not withdraw from the world, but you do need to choose to place your hand in His so that He is your constant companion on your journey. As you are refreshed by His fellowship, you will be able to live in the world as His child. Dwelling in His presence will strengthen your spirit, enabling you to say with David, "The LORD is my light and my salvation; whom shall I fear?" (Ps. 27:1 NKJV).

The prophetess Anna, widowed at a young age, went to dwell in the house of the Lord. Her continual prayers and service in the temple resulted in her chance to see Jesus when Joseph and Mary came to the temple to offer their sacrifice. This is our reward: seeing Jesus when we choose to abide with Him.

THE STRENGTHENING POWER OF ABIDING

David's purpose in abiding was to see the Lord's beauty. He just wanted to meditate on God's holiness, grace, mercy, faithfulness, and righteousness. He wanted to focus on the attributes of his God and delight in His character. That he did well, for his psalms give

ample evidence of his beholding the beauty of the Lord. Listen to
Psalm 145:

> The LORD is gracious and full of compassion,
> Slow to anger and great in mercy.
> The LORD is good to all,
> And His tender mercies are over all His works. (vv. 8–9 NKJV)

Those thoughts could be uttered only by one whose desire was to
see the loveliness of the Lord.

David also wanted to inquire of the Lord. He longed to inves-
tigate, to know, the ways of God and His dealings with His children. "Show me Your ways, O LORD," he asked. "Teach me Your
paths" (Ps. 25:4 NKJV). As he meditated on, inquired after, and listened to the Lord, he concluded that "the LORD is righteous in all
His ways, gracious in all His works" (Ps. 145:17 NKJV).

David's example of abiding teaches us to linger in the Lord's
presence so that we may become more intimately acquainted with
Him. It teaches us to ask for understanding and acceptance of His
will and ways.

The outcome of such closeness is security. We will grow confi-
dent in God's protection and strength during times of trouble.
David's consistent abiding prepared him inwardly to persevere. In
Psalm 18 he testified, "For by You I can run against a troop, by my
God I can leap over a wall" (v. 29 NKJV).

Paul experienced the Lord in a similar way, for he wrote to the
Philippians, "I can do all things through Christ who strengthens
me" (Phil. 4:13 NKJV).

To cultivate this inner courage requires us to abide consistently,
beholding the beauty of the Lord. Constant communion with our
Father provides assurance that He is our shield, that He will set us
high on a rock during difficulties.

Someone has commented that God does not always deliver out
of trouble, but He does deliver from the evil of trouble.[2] God pro-

vides safety by hiding us or shielding us inwardly. The assurance of being set high on a rock doesn't mean that the swirling waters will stop, but if we are on a rock, they will not sweep us away.

Years ago I whispered to the Lord that what mattered most to me was my relationship with Him. I told Him that for the rest of my life I wanted to abide in His presence. My priority in life now is to abide. Some days go by, and it seems that all I have really accomplished is spending some time sitting at the feet of Jesus. But as empty as these days may be from the world's viewpoint, I have accomplished the most necessary, the most important, the primary activity on my "do list."

Abiding does not guarantee that life will go smoothly. However, as David encouraged us in this psalm, it will ensure God's protection and strength.

I remember a time when I was complaining to the Lord about my life. In my heart, the Lord challenged me, *Okay, Cynthia, if you could do anything you wanted to do, what would you choose?* I thought about it for a long while. The more I thought, the more I realized that I didn't want anything to change. I wanted to continue to do David's one thing. I wanted to seek His face and His ways and then trust Him with my life. I wanted to say with Paul: "No, dear friends, I am still not all I should be, but I am focusing all my energies on this one thing: Forgetting the past and looking forward to what lies ahead, I strain to reach the end of the race and receive the prize for which God, through Christ Jesus, is calling us up to heaven" (Phil. 3:13–14 NLT).

> When the habit of inwardly gazing Godward becomes fixed within us we shall be ushered onto a new level of spiritual life more in keeping with the promises of God and the mood of the New Testament. The Triune God will be our dwelling place even while our feet walk the low road of simple duty here among men. We will have found life's *summum bonum* indeed.
>
> —A. W. Tozer[3]

For Reflection

Read Psalm 27:4–5. Why do you think the psalmist felt that dwelling with the Lord would ensure his safety?

Spend some time in prayer with this question: What is the one thing you want to ask of the Lord?

KEY THOUGHT FOR DEEPER INTIMACY: *Seeking constant communion with my Father ensures a consistent intimacy with Him.*

The Father speaks *(what is He saying to you?):*

The child responds *(what are you saying to Him?):*

PART THREE

The Father's Faithful Presence

THE FATHER AND THE CHILD

The Father spoke:
My child, are your times in prayer a blessing to you?

Yes, Father, it helps me to know that all I really need to do is to come to You with a loving heart. I am becoming more dependent upon Your Spirit and Your Word as I pray.

You know that I am with you in our times in secret, but I want to be present in all of your life.

I know You do, but it is so easy for me to forget to rely on You and to make my own decisions.

If only you knew how much I want to guide you, strengthen you, and protect you as you journey!

Father, teach me how to trust You with all my heart.

Keep seeking My kingdom and listening to My voice. Trust Me to strengthen you when you encounter trials, weariness, and attacks from the enemy. I am Your Shepherd, and I am committed to caring for you if you will let Me.

Thank You, Father; I want You to lead me and to be with me always.

That is my desire, too, My child. Take My hand. You may encounter some deep waters, but you will not be alone. I will be holding you close.

15

He Is with Me in Life's Deep Waters

When you pass through the waters, I will be with you;
And through the rivers, they shall not overflow you.
When you walk through the fire, you shall not be burned,
Nor shall the flame scorch you.

—*Isaiah 43:2 NKJV*

Few things are more uncomfortable than being sick away from home. On one trip I came down with a bad case of the flu. A dear friend brought her vaporizer for me to use at the retreat center where I was staying. The machine was powerful. It didn't emit soft, translucent wisps that quickly disappeared. The dense vapor it put out was thick and white. The display captivated me, and since I could do nothing else, I began to notice the varied types of soothing steam that drifted toward me.

At that point I thought of James's observation concerning the brevity of life: "For what is your life? It is even a vapor that appears for a little time and then vanishes away" (James 4:14 NKJV). I had always wanted to time a vapor to see just how long it lasted. Here was the perfect opportunity!

Armed with my watch, which had a second hand, and plenty of time for my research, I embarked on a highly scientific survey of the life of a vapor. I carefully chose the strongest vapors and soon became proficient in counting the seconds it took for the mist to dissipate. I now share with you my never-before-published results. Based on random samplings throughout the afternoon, I arrived at the conclusion that a vapor's longest life is seven seconds.

It thrilled me to have this information. Conducting that study had put my life in perspective in light of eternity. The seventy or so years I will dwell on the earth are only *seven seconds* compared with the everlasting, unending life I will have in heaven.

The knowledge of how truly momentary earthly life is encourages me to persevere through the deep waters and fiery trials I encounter on my journey. As Paul wrote, "For our present troubles are quite small and won't last very long" (2 Cor. 4:17 NLT). How true. And now I know how long—only a few seconds!

In the opening verse of Isaiah 43, before the comforting promise in verse 2 of God's faithful presence in trials, the Lord tenderly tells His children that they are His—He formed them, He redeemed them, and He called them by name. This affirming truth is necessary in order for children to trust a Father's companionship during hard times. As a loving Father, God assures His children of His commitment to stay by their side as they journey. As a wise Father, He tells His loved ones they will encounter deep waters and fire. These trials might cause them to lose heart without the support and strength of a Father.

You Will Have Trials

The first word in Isaiah 43:2 is *when,* not *if.* Apparently, trials are not an option. They are a given reality for all people, those who are redeemed and those who are not. Jesus indicated this reality when He said, "For He makes His sun rise on the evil and on the good, and sends rain on the just and on the unjust" (Matt. 5:45 NKJV). A friend wrote me a note saying that for some reason, we think since we're Christians we should get a discount on suffering! Although we don't know how deep the waters might be or how intense the flames, we do know that as God's children we can be certain of His protection *when* we pass through them.

Notice that the wording in this verse specifies that we will pass *through* the waters and walk *through* the fire. We must endure the difficulty, but our hope is based in the knowledge that we will come out on the other side. We can persevere and actually make progress through our trials.

Encouraging testimony to this truth came from the prophet Habakkuk: "He makes my feet like hinds' feet, and will make me to walk [not to stand still in terror, but to walk] *and* make [spiritual] progress upon my high places [of trouble, suffering or responsibility]!" (3:19 AMPLIFIED). We must all endure affliction, but God can use whatever we go through for our spiritual growth. Therefore, Paul exclaimed, "So we're not giving up. How could we! Even though on the outside it often looks like things are falling apart on us, on the inside, where God is making new life, not a day goes by without his unfolding grace" (2 Cor. 4:16 *Message*).

Two years ago I was facing surgery, an unwelcome interruption in my life. I remember thinking, *Yes, I will experience pain and need to spend time recuperating, but I have hope that if everything goes as planned, I can cross this small river in just a few weeks.* I knew that one way or another, I would get past this challenge and continue with my life. I would learn much during this time, but it would be a "passing through" experience.

GOD WILL BE WITH YOU

As we are passing through, the Lord tells us, "I will be with you." How incredible! What precious words! *I will be with you at all times; I will be with you when no one else can be with you. I will never leave you or forsake you.*

While reading about the early Christians who were martyred in Rome, I was struck by their courage. Such fearlessness could be attributed only to God's presence with them:

The faithful, while they were dragged along, proceeded with cheerful steps; their countenances shone with much grace and glory; their bonds were as the most beautiful ornaments; and they themselves looked as brides adorned with their richest array, breathing the fragrance of Christ. They were put to death in various ways: or, in other words, they wove a chaplet of various odours and flowers, and presented it to the Father.[1]

The dear martyrs must have had Psalm 23:4 (NLT) on their lips:

Even when I walk
   through the dark valley of death,
I will not be afraid,
   for you are close beside me.

We don't have to look far to witness examples of God's faithful presence in life's difficulties. When everyone else had deserted Paul at his first defense, the Lord was with him: "But the Lord stood with me and strengthened me" (2 Tim. 4:17 NKJV). A friend told me how she had prayed for safety as her daughter and her family drove to be with them at Christmas. On the way, there was a traffic accident, and her daughter was permanently injured. My friend asked God why He hadn't heard her prayer. His answer to her was, "But I did hear your prayer. I was with her, just as I have been with you." In this life we will pass through deep waters, but we will not be alone.

You Will Not Be Destroyed

God tells us that as we go through the rivers, we will not drown. Whatever our trials, we will be able to endure. The Lord sets limits on the rivers we must cross; the waters will not overflow us. As I see news reports of terrible flooding around the world, I think of this verse. Homes, cars, and businesses may be destroyed, but the ones who are in His will persevere in their spirits.

The protective intervention of God is clearly visible in the life of Job. As terrible as was Job's suffering, God set a hedge around him. The Lord limited Satan's power over Job; Satan could touch Job, but he was not allowed to take his life.

What a great comfort it is to know that our Father understands our frailty. He knows us better than we know ourselves, and He controls our circumstances. His grace is sufficient for living as we wade through deep waters, or for death when the number of our days has been completed.

I have often thought that the phrase "when you walk through the fire" should be worded "when you *run* through the fire." But here, God assures us that when we walk through the fire, we will not be scorched. Shadrach, Meshach, and Abednego were authorities on whether the fire will burn. As the objects of Nebuchadnezzar's wrath, they were thrown into a furnace, where they discovered the truth of Isaiah 43:2. The Lord was with them in the flames, and they were safe: "Then the princes, prefects, governors, and advisers crowded around them and saw that the fire had not touched them. Not a hair on their heads was singed, and their clothing was not scorched. They didn't even smell of smoke!" (Dan. 3:27 NLT).

Having gone through severe trials, the psalmist wrote, "We went through fire and flood. But you brought us to a place of great abundance" (Ps. 66:12 NLT). Another psalmist observed,

When they walk through the Valley of Weeping,
　　it will become a place of refreshing springs,
　　where pools of blessing collect after the rains! (Ps. 84:6 NLT)

Persevering brings abundant blessing. A young woman told me about a particularly trying circumstance she had been through and commented, "It was the hardest and the best thing I ever did." It was far from easy, but because she had gone through it, her experience became a place of refreshing springs.

After giving a speech in which I announced my findings

concerning the longevity of vapors, I received this thought in the mail: "Thank you for sharing about life essentially lasting only seven seconds. I want you to know that I plan to spend my remaining three-and-a-half seconds deepening my intimacy with God."

How about you, dear friend? I pray you are willing to take hold of your Father's hand and say, "Lord, I know You are with me. I know I might encounter deep waters and fiery furnaces along my journey, but I am comforted by Your promise to be with me. I want my few seconds here to bring You glory and to prepare me for my eternal home with You."

> No darkness is so deep, but white
> Wings of the angels through can pierce;
> *Nor any chain such heaps lies in*
> *But God's own hand can hold it light;*
> Nor is there any flame so fierce
> But Christ Himself can stand therein.
>
> —Amy Carmichael[2]

For Reflection

How do you know God is with you when you cross the rivers and walk through the fire?

Share with the Lord your feelings about His presence with you.

KEY THOUGHT FOR DEEPER INTIMACY: *I am never closer to my Father than when I pass through the waters or walk through the fire.*

The Father speaks *(what is He saying to you?)*:

The child responds *(what are you saying to Him?)*:

16

He Strengthens Me to Resist Sin

Remember that the temptations that come into your life are no different from what others experience. And God is faithful. He will keep the temptation from becoming so strong that you can't stand up against it. When you are tempted, he will show you a way out so that you will not give in to it.

—*1 Corinthians 10:13* NLT

*F*irst Corinthians 10:13 is one of the first verses I committed to memory. It is an anchor verse of the soul. The Spirit has whispered its truth in my heart many times: *Cynthia, you are not the only one ever to face this temptation. You have the power to stand firm because of God's faithfulness and your dependence upon Him. He carefully watches over you, and He will not allow anything to come into your life that you cannot bear.*

As I look back over the years, I can testify to the faithfulness of God in fulfilling this promise. He was always there to offer a way of escape, although there was sometimes debate about whether I *wanted* the way out. Every time I yielded to temptation, I was always able to look back and see how I could have resisted.

Just as trials are a normal part of life, so are temptations. No one on the journey to God's heart is exempt. Temptations are part of our common lot. Since the Garden of Eden, Satan has been able to offer enticing fruit to all who linger and listen. We are not to be *of* this world, but we are certainly *in* it. The world cries out to us from every corner. Opportunities to indulge and gratify the flesh abound.

Many years ago I heard a speaker say he had always thought the narrow road Christians were to travel was a little secluded path somewhere in the wilderness. It wasn't long, though, before he concluded that the narrow way was right in the middle of a broad freeway—going against the traffic!

There is comfort, however, in knowing that God is fully aware of our situation and has already provided a way out. We are not alone in dealing with temptation. Peter warned,

> Be careful! Watch out for attacks from the Devil, your great enemy. He prowls around like a roaring lion, looking for some victim to devour. Take a firm stand against him, and be strong in your faith. Remember that Christians all over the world are going through the same kind of suffering you are. (1 Peter 5:8–9 NLT)

Countless others have had to battle Satan, and countless Christians have taken firm stands against the devil. Our Lord was not exempt from Satan's attacks: "For we do not have a High Priest who cannot sympathize with our weaknesses, but was in all points tempted as we are, yet without sin" (Heb. 4:15 NKJV). Our Lord understands and is committed to enabling us to be strong.

HIS FAITHFULNESS, NOT YOUR STRENGTH

The difficulty with temptation is how tempting it is! Left to our own strength, we easily yield. But our God is faithful as we encounter temptation. He indwells us by His Holy Spirit, who immediately comes to our aid, empowers us, and guides us in the way of escape.

I experience God's faithfulness whenever I am tempted to take a minivacation and indulge myself in some unedifying form of relief. The Spirit speaks to me clearly about the decision I face, and

He is there to enable me to do what is right. Then it becomes my choice whether or not to obey.

I heard someone observe, "Most people want to be delivered from temptation but would still like it to keep in touch." William Gurnall, a wonderful Puritan writer in the seventeeth century, pointedly instructed us:

> Temptation is never stronger than when relief seems to dress itself in the very sin that Satan is suggesting . . . If we lean out the window to hear temptation's serenade, Satan is satisfied that his suit may in time be granted. If we do not wish to yield to sin, we must take care not to walk by or sit at the door of the occasion. Do not look on temptation with a wandering eye if you do not wish to be taken by it, nor allow your mind to dwell on that which you do not want lodged in your heart.[1]

The promise of God's faithfulness in enabling us to overcome the enemy's enticements comes into play only when we *want* to escape the temptation. This principle is evident in the life of the Proverbs 31 woman. The Scriptures tell us that she "does not eat the bread of idleness" (v. 27 NKJV). This phrase is coupled with her watching the ways of her household, and it refers to her diligence in taking care of her family and home. I believe this verse is describing not just her at-home activities, but also her constant vigilance in making sure that nothing comes into her life that will compromise her walk with God. She is a woman who first and foremost fears the Lord.

BUT THE CHOICE IS UP TO YOU

All that is necessary for our deliverance is our decision not to yield to temptation. Consider the contrasting stories of Lot's wife and of Joseph. When God sent the angels to destroy Sodom and Gomorrah, He singled out Lot and his family for rescue. Lot and his daughters obeyed the angels by not looking back on their city, but Lot's wife turned around to look with longing. In doing so she rejected God's rescue and was destroyed. God was faithful, but she was not. In contrast, Joseph said no to Potiphar's wife. Because the Lord was with him and he did not want to sin against God, he was able to flee from her daily seduction attempts. Peter told us that God can and will rescue us: "The Lord knows how to deliver the godly out of temptations" (2 Peter 2:9 NKJV).

For believers, all temptations are resistible. Since the power of sin has been broken in our lives, we have the choice of yielding ourselves to righteousness. Paul confirmed, "Our old sinful selves were crucified with Christ so that sin might lose its power in our lives. We are no longer slaves to sin" (Rom. 6:6 NLT).

We must understand the source of our temptations. The enemy is the one who assails us, and yielding to sin is our own decision. Scripture reminds us that "God is never tempted to do wrong, and he never tempts anyone else either. Temptation comes from the lure of our own evil desires" (James 1:13–14 NLT). In becoming new creations, we are given the ability to say no to sin. Satan cannot force us to yield because his power is limited: "He who is in you is greater than he who is in the world" (1 John 4:4 NKJV).

Just as God will not let the rivers overflow us or the fire consume us, so He will not allow a test or temptation to impose more than we can bear. As our Father, He carefully watches over all that comes into our lives. Our part is to trust Him for His grace and to find our security in His ability to sustain us. This belief will enable us to stand firm, resist, or flee as the Lord directs in each circumstance.

As we grasp the knowledge that whatever comes into our lives will not overpower us, we will find it easier to trust God's commitment to set a hedge around us. We can escape, and we can persevere. Paul, a battle-scarred veteran of tests and trials, wrote, "We are pressed on every side by troubles, but we are not crushed and broken. We are perplexed, but we don't give up and quit. We are hunted down, but God never abandons us. We get knocked down, but we get up again and keep going" (2 Cor. 4:8–9 NLT).

Life is not easy. It is full of trials and temptations. I think God knows we probably could not bear more than seven seconds! In our fleeting span, all of us will go through rivers, fire, and temptations. Wouldn't you rather go through them with God as your Protector and Shield? God is faithful to keep you from sin. His grace is sufficient for all your trials. As your Father, He longs to hold you close, especially when you are tempted.

> Where can anyone flee in any need, or when in danger of sin, Satan, or his instruments, except to God? . . . When you take sanctuary in God, you can rest assured He will not betray you to the enemy. Your willing dependence upon Him awakens His almighty power for your defense as surely as a newborn's cry awakens its mother, regardless of the hour. He has sworn the greatest oath that can come from His sacred lips; that all who flee to their hope in Him for refuge, shall have strong consolation (Heb. 6:17–18). This should embolden your faith to expect a kind haven when you turn to God for protection. Having set up His name and promises as a strong tower, God calls His people into His chambers, and expects them to enter and make themselves at home.
>
> —William Gurnall[2]

For Reflection

How does the promise of God's faithfulness in 1 Corinthians 10:13 help in times of temptation?

Turn this verse into a prayer you can offer when seeking God's strength to flee temptation.

KEY THOUGHT FOR DEEPER INTIMACY: *Knowing that my Father will protect and guide me during times of temptation draws me closer to Him.*

The Father speaks *(what is He saying to you?):*

The child responds *(what are you saying to Him?):*

17

He Prepares Me for Life's Struggles

In conclusion, be strong in the Lord—be empowered through your union with Him; draw your strength from Him—that strength which His [boundless] might provides. Put on God's whole armor—the armor of a heavy-armed soldier, which God supplies—that you may be able successfully to stand up against [all] the strategies and the deceits of the devil.

—Ephesians 6:10–11 AMPLIFIED

I remember feeling thrilled as I watched Charlton Heston compete in the furious chariot races in the movie *Ben-Hur*. The epic movie provided a spectacle of life in the Roman Empire. I was always impressed by the varied but practical pieces of armor worn by the Roman soldiers.

I used to read Ephesians 6:10–11 with these images in mind, trying to connect the classic Roman attire I'd seen on screen with what Paul was urging us to put on. Questions were always popping up: *Why do I need armor? Where do I get it? Exactly what is it that I am to put on, and how? Can others see it? Can I tell if I am missing a piece? Once I put on the armor, then what do I do?*

In concluding his letter to the Ephesians, Paul prefaced his discussion of spiritual armor with the exhortation: "Be strong in the Lord." We are not to attempt to be strong in our own power. If we are to resist temptation and stand against a deceitful enemy, we must receive all that the Lord provides for our conflict with Satan.

God has prepared for us armor, a defensive covering for the body to be used in combat. It is *God's* armor because He alone knows how to equip His children effectively for protection. Because he is ruler of the kingdom of darkness, Satan's goal is to defeat those who belong to the kingdom of light. The whole world lies in the power of the evil one, but the universe lies in the power of our almighty God. For the time that the evil one is allowed to rule, we must use God's armor and His strength to withstand Satan's attacks. Paul explained, "We are human, but we don't wage war with human plans and methods. We use God's mighty weapons, not mere worldly weapons, to knock down the Devil's strongholds" (2 Cor. 10:3–4 NLT). Our battle is spiritual, so we must use spiritual weapons.

To be strong in the Lord, we are told to put on the whole armor of God. Paul wrote to the Romans, "Therefore let us cast off the works of darkness, and let us put on the armor of light" (13:12 NKJV). The armor of light is sturdy kingdom clothing that not only protects us, but also exemplifies Christlike character.

This armor enables us to *stand* so that we do not fall under Satan's power. It has been observed that nothing but cowardice can lose the victory. James instructed, "So humble yourselves before God. Resist the Devil, and he will flee from you" (James 4:7 NLT). As we humbly accept our weakness and place our dependence upon the Lord by putting on His armor, we are ready to resist and stand firm.

ANATOMY OF A SUIT OF ARMOR

What is the armor with which we are to gird ourselves for spiritual battle? What is it composed of?

The belt of truth. In Paul's day, soldiers wore flowing robes. To be unencumbered while fighting, they needed to wear a belt to secure the excess material. The belt was a critical piece of armor because without it a soldier had no freedom of movement.

We are to put on knowledge of and belief in the truth of the gospel. We must embrace this truth with sincerity and a good conscience. It is precious to us; without it we will be hindered from living freely. Jesus Himself is the truth: "And you will know the truth, and the truth will set you free" (John 8:32 NLT). We know the truth about ourselves, God, and Satan. Truth encompasses us and gives us freedom to love, to trust, and to take a stand. We fight against an enemy of lies with a God of truth as the source of our strength.

The breastplate of righteousness. The breastplate defends the vital parts of the body, primarily the heart. Paul described the source of this righteousness in Philippians 3:8–9 (NKJV): "That I may gain Christ and be found in Him, not having my own righteousness, which is from the law, but that which is through faith in Christ, the righteousness which is from God by faith."

This righteousness is not our own good behavior. The Pharisees thought they were righteous, and they came under our Lord's severest criticism. This is the righteousness that is ours when we believe on the Lord Jesus Christ:

> It is emphatically *"the righteousness,"* so perfect that it satisfied every demand of Law, and is perfectly proof against all assaults from within or from without. Let us not show the bare breast of our righteousness to the tempter, but rather the righteousness of God himself, imputed to us and received by faith. This breastplate was purchased by Christ at a dear rate; none are his soldiers who have not put it on.[1]

Feet shod with the preparation of the gospel of peace. Soldiers had special military shoes equipped with nails on the soles for firm footing. For Christian soldiers, our shoes prepare our feet to stand firm on the gospel of peace and to be ready to march with this gospel. Perhaps if our feet are walking in the good news of Jesus Christ, then we would not wander into places or situations that would make us compromise the gospel in our lives. If our feet are shod with the gospel, then the good news is our mission, and wherever we go, the gospel goes with us.

The shield of faith. The Roman shield was large. It was a piece of lightweight wood, four feet long by two and a half feet wide. This shield, used to defend the whole body, was usually covered with linen and leather and oiled to withstand arrows, especially fiery ones. Wherever we are being attacked (whether it is aimed at the head, feet, or heart), we can use the shield of faith to quench all the fiery darts of the wicked one.

A soldier with a shield feels secure. So it is that our faith protects us as nothing else. It is indispensable in battle: "For every child of God defeats this evil world by trusting Christ to give the victory. And the ones who win this battle against the world are the ones who believe that Jesus is the Son of God" (1 John 5:4–5 NLT). Faith comes to our aid in every attack. Our faith is in God, who strengthens us and provides for our protection. David acknowledged God's protection by saying, "But you, O LORD, are a shield around me, my glory, and the one who lifts my head high" (Ps. 3:3 NLT).

The helmet of salvation. Our heads are most vulnerable. It was imperative that a soldier's head be guarded from enemy blows. Most helmets were made of thick leather or brass and adorned with a plume or crest. The helmet we are to put on is the hope of salvation. First Thessalonians 5:8 (NLT) tells us, "But let us who live in the light think clearly, protected by the body armor of faith and love, and wearing as our helmet the confidence of our salvation." Knowing that the victory is ours makes all the difference in the way we fight. Our hope is well founded. The assurance of our salvation keeps us clearheaded, no longer susceptible to doubt or despair from the enemy.

The sword of the Spirit. The sword of the Spirit is the Word of God. For the Roman soldier it was a two-edged dagger, and it was an essential piece of armor. We are told in Hebrews 4:12 (NKJV), "The word of God is living and powerful, and sharper than any two-edged sword, piercing even to the division of soul and spirit, and of joints and marrow, and is a discerner of the thoughts and intents of the heart." That was the weapon Jesus used against Satan when He was tempted in the wilderness. Each time He was tempted, He answered with a Scripture by saying, "It is written . . ." (Matt. 4:4, 7, 10).

Albert Barnes makes this observation concerning the temptation in the Garden of Eden: "Had Eve adhered simply to the word of God, and urged his command, without attempting to *reason* about it, she would have been safe."[2]

This is a powerful lesson for us. Can we use the Scriptures as expertly as a soldier can use a dagger in defending his life in battle? Psalm 119:11 (NLT) is most applicable here: "I have hidden your word in my heart, that I might not sin against you."

Each piece of the armor is a powerful weapon for employment in our warfare. One of my problems, though, is that I have never really understood *how* to put on the armor and *how* to know if I had it on! I asked the Lord to help me understand how to be fully armored. The thought came to my heart that if I am consistently abiding in Christ, then I will have the whole armor of God. To abide is to constantly be connected to Christ. He is the Vine; I am the branch. Christ is the *truth,* He is our *righteousness,* He is the *gospel of peace,* He is the Author and Finisher of our *faith,* He is our *salvation,* and the Scriptures are the *Word of God.*

As we sit at the Lord's feet each day and listen to His Word with a heart to obey, we will stay completely armored. Essentially, we are never to take off the armor, for we are to stay alert and vigilant because of our adversary, the devil. It will be in our abiding that we can discover any weak part of our armor.

As you "put on the Lord Jesus Christ," you have on the whole armor of God. You are empowered through your union with Him and are able to successfully stand up against all the strategies and deceits of the devil. When you are covered with His provision, you are safe within your Father's embrace.

Doubt your own strength, but never doubt Christ's . . . Christian, take special care not to trust in the armour of God, but in the *God* of the armour. All your weapons are only "mighty through God" [2 Cor. 10:4].

—William Gurnall[3]

For Reflection

Why is the armor mentioned in Ephesians 6:10–11 necessary for the Christian?

Ask God to supply His armor and the strength you need to stand firm.

KEY THOUGHT FOR DEEPER INTIMACY: *Putting on the full armor of God ensures my Father's closeness.*

The Father speaks *(what is He saying to you?)*:

The child responds *(what are you saying to Him?)*:

18

He Guides Me Through Life

Lean on, trust and be confident in the Lord with all your heart
and mind, and do not rely on your own insight or understanding.
In all your ways know, recognize and acknowledge Him, and He
will direct and make straight and plain your paths.

—*Proverbs 3:5–6 AMPLIFIED*

I clearly remember an occasion on which I was crossing a busy
street with our oldest daughter, who was then three years old.
"Hold my hand," I urged her.

"I hold my own hand!" she replied.

It is no different when our heavenly Father extends His hand
to guide us through life. We think we can find our own way across
the landscape. We don't need anyone bigger or wiser than we are;
we can take care of ourselves. We like to make our own judgment
calls, the adult version of holding our own hands.

After His children were enslaved for four hundred years, God
led them out of Egypt. He had heard their cries, and He sent Moses
as their deliverer. God's plan was for them to go on a few days'
march to a land He had prepared for them, flowing with milk and
honey. He was pleased to bless His children with the good land as
a permanent home. He was directing and making their paths
straight.

But the Israelites did not trust in the Lord with all their hearts, and consequently, they chose not to enter Canaan. That generation, who relied on their own understanding, spent their remaining days following circuitous paths in the wilderness.

These few words, *trust in the Lord with all your heart,* express a most profound and foundational truth for a child of God. All the Lord asks is that we *trust*—rely on, have faith in, depend upon, believe—in Him. This is an incredibly simple and commonsense request, but it seems to require an almost herculean effort to comply. Here is the God of the universe—*everything* exists by His power—and we, as His beloved children, struggle with trusting Him with our lives.

We are asked to trust with *all* the heart. Halfhearted trust is not trust. Once when I was challenged to trust the Lord implicitly, I told Him that I would be glad to trust Him if I knew what He had planned! Gently but clearly, He made known to me that trust is wholehearted and unconditional.

The psalmist assured the Lord of his undivided loyalty:

> With my whole heart I have sought You . . .
> Give me understanding, and I shall keep Your law;
> Indeed, I shall observe it with my whole heart. (Ps. 119:10,
> 34 NKJV)

Wholeheartedness denotes a solid commitment to seek and obey the Lord without reservation. Jesus referred to being halfhearted as *lukewarm* (Rev. 3:16 NKJV), something that was offensive to Him. If we are to trust the Lord, it must be a full-fledged, unqualified surrender.

DON'T BE IMPRESSED WITH YOURSELF

When we are asked to trust in the Lord, we are specifically asked *not* to trust in ourselves. "Don't be impressed with your own wisdom," Solomon cautioned (Prov. 3:7 NLT). Isaiah warned, "Destruction is certain for those who think they are wise and consider themselves to be clever" (Isa. 5:21 NLT).

The Scriptures are filled with examples of people who did precisely what God tells us *not* to do. Eve relied on her own wisdom when she ate the fruit. The Israelites relied on their own insight when they refused to enter Canaan. The disciples thought it best to tell Jesus to send the multitudes away when it was getting late.

How presumptuous of us to assume that we know better than God. We are limited by our finite perspectives; we cannot begin to fathom the wisdom or ways of God. It is hard for us to give up our understanding for His, but not doing so is like traveling to the Grand Canyon, stopping at only one lookout point, and then going away thinking we have seen the entire canyon. So much more awaits us. As Paul exclaimed, "Oh, what a wonderful God we have! How great are his riches and wisdom and knowledge! How impossible it is for us to understand his decisions and his methods! For who can know what the Lord is thinking? Who knows enough to be his counselor?" (Rom. 11:33–34 NLT).

The Israelites refused to enter the promised land because they were looking through the lenses of their own understanding. Then they proceeded to judge whether or not God was wise in where He was taking them. After all, why would He want them to enter a land that was filled with well-fortified cities and populated by the descendants of Anak, who were as big as giants?

Yet they were questioning the very God who had just mightily delivered them from bondage to Pharaoh, who had divided an entire sea for them to cross and closed it back up over their enemies, and who had provided food and water for the whole nation. Still they could not say, "What a wonderful God we have! It's impossible to understand His decisions or methods, but He loves us and He is trustworthy. Even though we aren't sure about what we see, we are sure of God. We will enter the land."

The real questions before us are not whether there are giants in the land, whether there is enough food to go around, or whether we can see far enough down the road to know if we ought to take that path. The only questions we have to answer are these: "Is God trustworthy? Is He faithful? Does He love us? Is He capable of orchestrating our lives for good? Is He sovereign?" If the answers are yes, then it is obvious we should not rely on our own understanding.

One reason I love this passage is that it's very clear. We don't need to sit around and discuss its theological implications: "I wonder what God means by *Do not rely on your own insight*?" All we need to do is to take God's outstretched hand.

ACKNOWLEDGE GOD WITH MIND AND HEART

Once we recognize the fruitlessness of relying on our own understanding, how do we know what to do? What does it mean to acknowledge God in all our ways?

To acknowledge means "to recognize, to notice, to know." It is not a studied knowledge, but an understanding that desires intimate acquaintance. It is to want God's will in *all* areas of our lives, not just *some* areas. We seek Him not just in the throes of crisis or during especially meaningful times of worship, but in all aspects of our lives. We ask Him to guide and direct us along *all* our paths, major and minor. We inquire of His will before making decisions instead of relying on what we think is right, seeking to understand with the mind and respond with the heart.

The apostle Paul exemplified the practice of acknowledging God in all our ways: "I myself no longer live, but Christ lives in me. So I live my life in this earthly body by trusting in the Son of God, who loved me and gave himself for me" (Gal. 2:20 NLT). Paul had abandoned his life to God. He spent the rest of his life—the *whole* of his life—in seeking, trusting, and proclaiming God in whatever he did. He testified to the treasure of such a life: "Yes, everything else is worthless when compared with the priceless gain of knowing Christ Jesus my Lord" (Phil. 3:8 NLT).

Many other Scripture writers testified to the importance of acknowledging God in all our choices. Jeremiah prayed, "O LORD, I know the way of man is not in himself; it is not in man who walks to direct his own steps" (Jer. 10:23 NKJV). Solomon taught that when we trust with all our hearts and acknowledge the Lord in all our ways, we will receive His guidance. David prayed,

> Teach me how to live, O LORD.
>> Lead me along the path of honesty [NASB, "level path"],
>> for my enemies are waiting for me to fall. (Ps. 27:11 NLT)

Derek Kidner comments on David's prayer, "He is very much in the world, and the prayer for a *level path* is not for comfort but for sure progress (as a moral term it implies what is right, or straight) when the merest slip would be exploited."[1]

God delights in leading us when we wholeheartedly seek His will. The result of our trust is that our paths are straight or level. This does not mean that the way is smooth or unhindered on our journey, but it does mean that we will not waste time wandering in the wildernesses of our own misguided decisions. Any path directed by the Lord will be much straighter and more level than one we might choose on our own.

Consider the story of Ruth, a young Moabite widow who chose to go with her mother-in-law to a foreign country and glean for the rest of her life. Why did she go? Certainly not because it seemed to be an exciting plan that promised personal fulfillment— quite the opposite. Ruth went with Naomi because she sought refuge under the wings of God (Ruth 2:12).

Ruth trusted God with all her heart to be her refuge, and she did not rely on her own insight. Had she done so, she would have stayed in the security of her own country with her family, where she had a promising future. Instead, she followed Naomi to Bethlehem and settled down to provide for them both by gleaning—menial and tiring labor, and risky for women. That she was known as a woman of virtue attests that she acknowledged God in all her ways.

Ruth's path was an honest one, but it was not particularly smooth. Her husband had died, she had moved to a new culture, and she had to work hard to support herself and her mother-in-law. But because she trusted God, the Scriptures say that she "happened" into the field of Boaz. The encounter was God's directing her path to meet the man she would eventually marry. Her straight path led her to fulfill God's plan: she and Boaz became the great-grandparents of David and were privileged to be in the lineage of Christ.

The best choice you can make for your life is to trust God with all your heart. The second best choice you can make is to determine not to rely on your own insight. As you seek to acknowledge God in all your ways, you will find your paths leading you into the center of His will and directly into His arms.

> Whenever you are doubtful as to your course, submit your judgment absolutely to the Spirit of God and ask Him to shut against you every door but the right one. Say, "Blessed Spirit, I cast on You the entire responsibility of closing against my steps any and every course that is not of God. Let me hear Your voice behind me whenever I turn to the right hand or the left. Put Your restraint on me. Do not allow me to go my own way."

> In the meanwhile, continue along the path that you have been already treading. It lies in front of you; pursue it. Abide in the calling in which you were called. Keep on as you are unless you are clearly told to do something else. Expect to have as clear a door out as you had in. If there is no indication to the contrary, consider the absence of indication to be the indication of God's will that you're on His track.

> —F. B. Meyer[2]

For Reflection

What does the Proverbs writer indicate are the keys to trusting God in 3:5–6?

Pray for discernment in knowing when you are relying on your own insight instead of trusting God.

KEY THOUGHT FOR DEEPER INTIMACY: *Trusting my Father with all my heart bonds my heart with His.*

The Father speaks *(what is He saying to you?)*:

The child responds *(what are you saying to Him?)*:

19

He Takes Care of Me

The LORD is my shepherd;
I shall not want.
He makes me to lie down in green pastures;
He leads me beside the still waters.

—*Psalm 23:1–2* NKJV

*N*ew Zealand is a country abounding in sheep. In fact, there are far more sheep than people! I had the privilege of visiting a sheep ranch on a recent trip. The owner showed us around his beautiful farmland and then took us over to the corral in which the sheep were penned. From a distance, the animals looked calm and seemed to be enjoying the sunny day.

As we approached the corral, the entire flock darted to one corner of the pen, pushing and shoving against the fence. The owner picked out a sheep and almost had to carry it over to us so we could pet it and show our affection.

As we were watching the nervous sheep, their shepherd appeared. He wore a typical Down Under hat, shorts, and boots, and he carried a rather tall shepherd's crook. He asked if we would like to see him and his dogs move the sheep from the pen to a pasture, and we eagerly assented.

It was quite an event. Once the sheep sensed that something

major was about to happen, they began milling about in one big clump, wild-eyed and snorting. Frightened of the unknown and distressed by the dogs' presence, some fifty sheep huddled in fear, ready to bolt at the next opportunity. When the gate was opened, they ran wildly in one group, headed in the wrong direction. The dogs barked, nipped at their heels, and turned them around. The shepherd gave certain calls, waved his arms and staff, and with the help of the dogs, drove the reluctant sheep to a spacious grazing pasture.

When David wrote the beloved Psalm 23, he drew on his experience as a shepherd to make insightful spiritual parallels for our lives. He didn't have Aussie sheepdogs, but he did have a shepherd's staff and many years of tending his flocks. He was well practiced in a shepherd's responsibilities, and he was acquainted firsthand with the nature of sheep. He lived with passion and conviction about the Father's presence in the lives of His children, likening it to a shepherd's watchful care over his sheep.

In the Care of a Personal Shepherd

The LORD is my shepherd. These are heartfelt words from one who had individually been protected and provided for by his Shepherd. Perhaps in the opening statement David was recalling his conquest of Goliath or the many occasions on which he had been saved from the wrath of Saul or the victories he had been granted over the Philistines or the restoration of his throne from Absalom. David had been through countless crises in which God intervened and defended him. There was no doubt of the divine Shepherd's presence.

David referred to the Lord as "*my* shepherd." David was divinely owned: he belonged to God, his personal Shepherd. On another occasion David proclaimed, "The LORD is *my* light and *my* salvation; whom shall I fear?" (Ps. 27:1 NKJV, emphasis added). His relationship with God was not casual; it was intensely intimate.

Because David understood God's commitment to shepherd him, he was confident that the Lord, as any good shepherd would do, would provide for all his needs. A shepherd was responsible to supply food, water, protection, and care for injuries. David would not lack for anything.

David was also aware that a good shepherd knows his sheep individually. He knows them by name, watches them carefully, and is attentive to any special needs. Phillip Keller, a contemporary author who is an experienced shepherd, comments, "Sheep do not 'just take care of themselves,' as some might suppose. They require, more than any other class of livestock, endless attention and meticulous care."[1] Having experienced God's gracious and constant care of him, David could sing confidently, *"I shall not want—now or in the future. I completely trust my Shepherd."*

AT REST IN THE FIELDS OF THE LORD

He makes me to lie down in green pastures. Sheep have to be made to lie down in green pastures. Phillip Keller explains that sheep will not lie down unless the shepherd makes it possible for them to rest, by ensuring they have these four requirements: freedom from fear, freedom from friction with other sheep, freedom from flies or parasites, and freedom from the fear of hunger.[2]

Sheep have little means of self-defense. The New Zealand sheep I observed were extremely timid, fearful of anything unexpected. If one sheep was scared and ran, then all the others ran too. Running is their main defense. What calms sheep more than anything is the presence of the shepherd. They feel safe and secure when he is with them.

We find it hard to rest if we are fearful. Over and over in Scripture, God comforts us with these consoling words: "Fear not, for I am with you" (see, for example, Isa. 41:10 NKJV). We will find relief from fear when we turn our gaze away from real or imagined threats and fix it on the constant presence of our divine Shepherd who provides for us and protects us.

Certainly, it is difficult to lie down if there is unresolved conflict. Keller recounts that when some sheep intimidated others, the rivalry stopped as soon as the shepherd appeared. His presence brought peace. When we embrace the Lord's presence in our lives, we can expect that He will promote peace and reconciliation.

A diligent shepherd takes great care in seeing that his sheep are free of pests, or else they will be continually bothered by all sorts of flies and ticks and will have to stamp their legs, shake their heads, or rush into bushes for relief. Problems, anxieties, and irritations keep us from resting with the Lord. "Don't worry about anything," Paul counseled. "Instead, pray about everything . . . [and] you will experience God's peace" (Phil. 4:6–7 NLT). As we cast our burdens upon the Lord by praying and releasing our anxieties, we will experience His peace.

Green pastures are essential for sheep to thrive and rest. Hungry sheep seldom rest, for they must stay in a continual search for food. Providing such pastures demands that the shepherd invest considerable time and strenuous labor, but he does it gladly because he wants the sheep to grow by eating and resting in these lush meadows.

This is also God's desire: that we grow spiritually by nourishing our souls with the food He provides and resting in Him. Charles Spurgeon thought that the green pastures refer to the Word of God: "Sweet and full are the doctrines of the gospel; fit food for souls, as tender grass is natural nutriment for sheep. When by faith we are enabled to find rest in the promises, we are like the sheep that lie down in the midst of the pasture."[3] The Scriptures are filled with images that support this interpretation. "Your words were found, and I ate them," declared Jeremiah. "And Your word was to me the joy and rejoicing of my heart" (15:16 NKJV). The Scriptures are rich, green pastures that feed our spirits and provide rest and refreshment: "Great peace have those who love Your law" (Ps. 119:165 NKJV).

When sheep lie down in green pastures, they *ruminate*—that is, they chew again what has been chewed slightly and swallowed. This process is necessary for the sheep to fully digest their food. *To ruminate* also means "to ponder, to reflect on, to chew on." This is what we are to do with the green pasture of the Word. We eat and then, in a time of quiet, meditate on its meaning for our lives.

The shepherd in New Zealand had to drive the sheep from a stuffy, hot pen to a green meadow. Although God does not force us to lie down, in His goodness He provides rest and refreshment. Just as a shepherd prepares the land to produce lush grass, so God has prepared everything we need for godly lives. He provides His Word and His Spirit, and through them, He gives us rest.

David's complete trust in the Lord enabled him to affirm that his Shepherd provided green pastures and still waters for his rest and refreshment. *The Message* renders these verses, "You have bedded me down in lush meadows, you find me quiet pools to drink from." Sheep are so skittish that rushing, noisy streams frighten them. Still waters calm and soothe them. Charles Spurgeon wrote of their soothing effect on our spirits:

> What are these "still waters" but the influences and graces of his blessed Spirit? His Spirit attends us in various operations, like waters—in the plural—to cleanse, to refresh, to fertilise, to cherish . . . Not to raging waves of strife, but to peaceful streams of holy love does the Spirit of God conduct the chosen sheep.[4]

The shepherd I met in New Zealand *drove* the sheep. Your Shepherd *leads* you beside still waters. He gently guides. He calls you to come to Him and receive rest. He is intimately acquainted with your nature and your needs because He is the perfect Shepherd. He invites you to follow Him willingly: "They will neither hunger nor thirst. The searing sun and scorching desert winds will not reach them anymore. For the LORD in his mercy will lead them beside cool waters" (Isa. 49:10 NLT).

Before our Lord Jesus could feed the people, He had to make them sit down. Before He can feed us we too must sit down.

David sat before the Lord; he was quiet before his God. Even if we have not a long time to spend in the morning with our God, much can be received in a very few minutes if only we are quiet. Sometimes it takes a little while to gather our scattered thoughts and quiet our soul. Even so, don't hurry; make it sit down on the green grass.

—Amy Carmichael[5]

For Reflection

What are the specific ways in your life that God provides what David described in Psalm 23:1–2 as "green pastures" and "still waters"?

Take some time in prayer to thank your personal Shepherd for His provision of your needs for rest and refreshment.

KEY THOUGHT FOR DEEPER INTIMACY: *The more I partake of the Father's provision for my rest and refreshment, the deeper my relationship with Him will be.*

The Father speaks *(what is He saying to you?):*

The child responds *(what are you saying to Him?):*

He Never
Leaves Me

He refreshes and restores my life—my self; He leads me in the paths of righteousness [uprightness and right standing with Him—not for my earning it, but] for His name's sake. Yes, though I walk through the [deep, sunless] valley of the shadow of death, I will fear or dread no evil; for You are with me; Your rod [to protect] and Your staff [to guide], they comfort me.

—*Psalm 23:3–4* AMPLIFIED

*B*irthdays are special occasions, especially when they mark a decade. I recently celebrated my sixtieth birthday, which thrust me into the category of "senior citizen." This reality hit home when I was dining in a restaurant and noticed that they offered a 10 percent discount for those sixty and over, which now applied to me!

On the day itself, a group of friends gave me a lovely surprise party. One of the things my children did to make the day special and to encourage me as I crossed this threshold was to present me with a gift certificate for a day at a Tucson spa. In the midst of what might have been a sobering event, I experienced refreshment, encouragement, and perspective.

Sometimes, events in life are so momentous that they weigh heavily upon us and the pressure does not seem to let up. It is easy to become overwhelmed or, as David lamented in Psalm 42:11 (NKJV), to feel that our souls have been "cast down." Author Phillip Keller has described caring for sheep who are "cast down"—they turn over on their backs and can't get up again without help.[1] This especially happens to heavier sheep who lie down in a hollowed-out piece of ground and roll over to get comfortable. Once their center of gravity shifts, they can't reverse it, and they are stuck in that position. Depending on the weather and how long it takes to find the sheep, the animal may die.

Keller looked diligently for any such "cast down" sheep, for the shepherd is the only one who can restore them. In his discouraged state, David knew well that the only answer to his soul's dilemma was to "hope in God" (Ps. 42:5 NKJV). The divine Shepherd is indeed our best source of restoration and refreshment.

HE RESTORES ME

David knew where he needed to go and who he needed to talk to when he was in despair:

> Listen to my prayer, O God.
>   Do not ignore my cry for help!
> Please listen and answer me,
>   for I am overwhelmed by my troubles. (Ps. 55:1–2 NLT)

Because David had continually cried out to the Lord and experienced His renewal, he could say simply and boldly, "He restores my life."

This restoration covered all circumstances, as Charles Spurgeon affirmed: "When the soul grows sorrowful he revives it; when it is sinful he sanctifies it; when it is weak he strengthens it."[2] After his sorrow, David could testify, "In Your presence is fullness of joy" (Ps. 16:11 NKJV). After repenting of sin, he could attest, "Blessed is he whose transgression is forgiven, whose sin is covered" (Ps. 32:1 NKJV). And after weakness, he could exclaim, "But the LORD was my support . . . It is God who arms me with strength" (Ps. 18:18, 32 NKJV).

Peter was a recipient of the resurrected Lord's tender restoration. The night of Jesus' arrest, Peter denied knowing Him. Afterward, he wept bitterly. When the risen Jesus met the disciples on the seashore, He spoke to the broken man. For each of the three times Peter had denied knowing Jesus, he was asked to affirm his love for the Lord. In that way, Peter was forgiven, restored, and commissioned to the ministry of the gospel as Jesus set him on the path of leading the church.

Our Good Shepherd looks for sheep who are laid low in order to restore, refresh, and revive each one. But in helping us stand, He also returns us to His chosen path. This path is always one of truth and righteousness, leading to our heavenly home. It is a safeguard against wandering in wrong directions. The Lord's restoration usually cultivates in us a deeper trust and a renewed desire for God to direct our ways.

The Lord's path of righteousness draws us into close fellowship with Him, for we are allowing Him to lead us. This right path is filled with blessings, as David affirmed: "For You, O LORD, will bless the righteous; with favor You will surround him as with a shield" (Ps. 5:12 NKJV). We still walk this path as imperfect travelers, but the more familiar it becomes to us, the more we will be intimate with our Shepherd.

HE LEADS ME THROUGH DARK VALLEYS

The paths of righteousness are filled with blessing and the Shepherd's presence, but they are not trouble free. Nevertheless, they are more desirable than any other paths the world has to offer: "A single day in your courts is better than a thousand anywhere else!" (Ps. 84:10 NLT).

Our Shepherd leads us for His name's sake—not for what we have done, but for who He is. He loves His sheep, and He desires to lead us on the right paths, for in doing so we bring glory and honor to His name.

David knew that the Shepherd's path led not only through restful meadows and by refreshing waters, but also through dark valleys shadowed by difficulty and death. Keller writes that in the summer, conscientious shepherds would lead their flocks up to the high country to graze. Usually, though, the best route up to the mountains was through the valleys, which contained "rampaging rivers, avalanches; rock slides; poisonous plants; the ravages of predators that raid the flock."[3]

David was aware of those dangers, for he had killed a lion and a bear while taking his sheep through deep ravines. As he led his sheep through the valley, he knew that there was no reason to fear because he, their shepherd, was with them and would protect them.

David's experience in leading his flock gave him bold confidence in speaking to his Shepherd. In the preceding verses, David was speaking *of* the Shepherd. Then as he addressed life's dangerous places, he began speaking *to* his Shepherd:

> Even when I walk
>   through the dark valley of death,
> I will not be afraid,
>   for you are close beside me. (Ps. 23:4 NLT)

According to A. F. Kirkpatrick, the Hebrew word translated "shadow of death" can also be rendered "deep gloom."[4] Another commentator echoes, "The word is applicable to any path of gloom or sadness; any scene of trouble or sorrow; any dark and dangerous way."[5] Whether the Scripture is referring to death or a dark and difficult trial, the glorious truth is that we will walk through it, and we will not be alone. These words paint a picture of walking at a steady pace through an unfamiliar region with one who knows the way. Having a trusted guide at your side alleviates all fear.

THE COMFORT OF THE SHEPHERD'S STAFF

One of the reasons David felt safe was that he took comfort in the Lord's rod and staff. The shepherd's rod is a wooden club—a symbol of authority employed to protect, defend, and correct the sheep. The shepherd uses it to drive off predators, to beat bushes in order to flush out snakes or other creatures that might disturb the flock, and to examine the sheep's fleece by separating the thick wool to detect any signs of trouble.

The shepherd's staff is long and slender, with a crook at one end. It is a unique tool, carried only by shepherds and used mainly to guide and comfort sheep. The crook enables the shepherd to draw individual sheep to him, especially timid ones. When a sheep gets caught in a bramble bush or slips down a cliff, he uses the crook to disentangle the animal or lift it up to safety. If there is a particularly wayward sheep, he reminds the animal to stay with the flock by gently laying the staff against the sheep's side to keep it on the right path. Often, a shepherd will extend the staff and simply touch a sheep's side as a reassuring sign of affection.[6]

No wonder David feared no evil! The Lord was well equipped to handle any emergency and to guide him safely on level paths or through difficult valleys. If predators attacked him with evil intent, the Lord would protect. If David wandered down the wrong path, the Lord would discipline him to bring him back. No matter what, the Lord would continually be guiding David, comforting him, and drawing him ever closer to his Shepherd's side. In another psalm David sang, "The LORD is my rock and my fortress and my deliverer . . . my shield . . . my stronghold" (Ps. 18:2 NKJV). No danger could overwhelm him; no discouragement could crush him. He was safe in his Shepherd's keeping.

What comfort there is in having a strong protector and guide to accompany you on every step of your journey! Earlier this year I went on an extended guided walk that traversed more than thirty-two miles across a variety of challenging terrain. "Walk" doesn't do it justice—it was actually a rugged and challenging hike! Our knowledgeable guide made the journey interesting by teaching us in depth about the geography of the region and the plant and animal life we saw. He made the walk enjoyable by taking full responsibility for us. He provided food and water, companionship, and even emergency medical treatment for our blisters. We didn't have to concern ourselves with anything except following him and staying on the path.

One day we climbed eleven switchbacks in order to reach a 3,500-foot pass from near sea level. As we kept putting one foot in front of the other—and breathing heavily!—our guide was there to keep us going with welcome encouragement. By the time we completed our trek, we felt quite close to him.

There are individuals who hike that particular trail without a guide, just as there are people who go through life alone. Given a choice, I would rather have an experienced guide to lead me, provide for my needs, encourage me, and protect me. As strenuous as the journey may be, I can be at rest along the way if I travel in the presence of a personal shepherd. David would agree. How about you?

Do not look forward to the changes and chances of this life in fear. Rather look at them with full hope that, as they arise, God, whose you are, will deliver you out of them. He has kept you hitherto; do you but hold fast to His dear hand, and He will lead you safely through all things; and when you cannot stand, He will bear you in His arms.

Do not look forward to what may happen tomorrow. The same everlasting Father who cares for you today will take care of you tomorrow, and every day. Either He will shield you from suffering, or He will give you unfailing strength to bear it. Be at peace, then; put aside all anxious thoughts and imaginations.

—Frances de Sales[7]

For Reflection

Based on Psalm 23:3–4, how would you characterize the qualities of a good shepherd?

Tell your Father your most urgent needs for His guidance and protection to keep you from wandering away from Him.

KEY THOUGHT FOR DEEPER INTIMACY: *As I allow my divine Shepherd to lead me along His paths, I will be comforted and kept close by His side, no matter how dark the valley.*

The Father speaks *(what is He saying to you?):*

The child responds *(what are you saying to Him?):*

21

He Strengthens Me When I Am Weary

He gives power to those who are tired and worn out; he offers strength to the weak. Even youths will become exhausted, and young men will give up. But those who wait on the LORD will find new strength. They will fly high on wings like eagles. They will run and not grow weary. They will walk and not faint.

—*Isaiah 40:29–31* NLT

*O*n the extended trek I undertook earlier this year, I experienced firsthand what it was like to walk until I was worn out. Even though I was exhilarated by the beauty we witnessed, by the middle of each day I couldn't wait until we quit for the day and I could take off my boots, put my feet up, and rest. Many times I thought I couldn't walk another step. During those times, I recalled this wonderful promise that those who wait on the Lord will "walk and not faint or become tired" (Isa. 40:31 AMPLIFIED). I was ready to know what it meant to wait for the Lord and experience His power.

Part of Isaiah's prophetic message to Israel was assurance of God's help and comfort during a period in which the exiled people felt that God had forgotten them. Isaiah prefaced these concluding verses of chapter 40 with the questions, "Have you not known? Have you not heard? The everlasting God, the Lord, the Creator of the ends of the earth, does not faint or grow weary; there is no searching of His understanding" (Isa. 40:28 AMPLIFIED). Israel was reminded that God's strength is inexhaustible, His wisdom unsearchable. He is not weak, like man.

When the pilgrims made their way to worship in Jerusalem, they would sing hymns from the Psalter. One of the passages they sang was this:

> He will not let you stumble and fall;
>   the one who watches over you will not sleep.
> Indeed, he who watches over Israel
>   never tires and never sleeps. (Ps. 121:3–4 NLT)

How could the exiles presume that the all-powerful Creator of the universe would lack the strength to protect His own children?

"Look around you!" the prophet urged the weary people, who in their fatigue and discouragement were questioning God. "See the heavens, the fruit of the earth, the imprint of the Lord's hand in the world day and night. Can you question His inscrutable wisdom or doubt that your eternally wakeful God is aware of your circumstances? He is your covenant God, faithful and sovereign. His ways are higher than yours. You will find your consolation not in the false gods you construct, but in the assurance of the wisdom and strength of the Holy One of Israel on your behalf."

Paul echoed this thought in the gospel he was inspired to preach: "This 'foolish' plan of God is far wiser than the wisest of human plans, and God's weakness is far stronger than the greatest of human strength" (1 Cor. 1:25 NLT). God gives power to the faint and weary, and He increases strength to those who are weak. What hope and encouragement are in these words!

THE SOURCE OF OUR STRENGTH

To rely on God's power, you must acknowledge your weakness and seek the strength only He can give. This is particularly challenging for those of us who tend toward self-reliance. David wonderfully modeled reliance on God rather than self. He was well practiced in asking God for His strength: "In the day when I cried out, You answered me, and made me bold with strength in my soul" (Ps. 138:3 NKJV). W. Clarkson comments, "God has access to our human souls—direct and immediate access. He can 'lay his hand upon us,' and touch the secret springs of our nature, calling forth all that is best and worthiest, 'strengthening us with strength in our soul.'"[1]

Adults will often exclaim upon observing active children, "Oh, how I wish I had their energy!" But youth is no guarantee of strength. Isaiah stated that even young men fall prey to exhaustion. The "faintness" described by the prophet is not a matter of age. The strength that God imparts is far different from the vitality of youth. This strength enables you to do *all* things. The Lord is essentially concerned about the strength of your spirit, although God is not limited in supplying physical strength when needed.

We are fortunate to have so many letters from Paul in the Scriptures because he was an authority on God's strength. Without divine power, he would never have survived the sufferings he was forced to endure. Listen to these words of testimony:

> Though our bodies are dying, our spirits are being renewed every day. (2 Cor. 4:16 NLT)

> I can do everything with the help of Christ who gives me the strength I need. (Phil. 4:13 NLT)

> Each time [the Lord] said, "My gracious favor is all you need. My power works best in your weakness." (2 Cor. 12:9 NLT)

Paul's teaching continually contrasted human weakness with divine strength.

In his prayers for believers, Paul frequently asked that they receive strength in their spirits. He prayed for the Ephesians "that from his glorious, unlimited resources he will give you mighty inner strength through his Holy Spirit" (3:16 NLT). The apostle had learned that the best way to live in God's strength was not to have any strength of his own. We tend to think of weakness as a failing or shortcoming. The good news from the Scriptures is that weakness is a prerequisite to spiritual strength. That is why God can "increase" strength, "causing it to multiply and making it abound" (Isa. 40:29 AMPLIFIED) in those who have grown faint and weary.

How do we receive God's strength? Isaiah provided a very important qualification: "those who wait for the Lord" (40:31 AMPLIFIED).

THE KEY TO RECEIVING HIS STRENGTH

Israel needed to understand God's desire and ability to give strength to His children. But Isaiah knew they also needed instruction in how to appropriate God's strength. After citing the frailty of youth, he immediately declared, "But those who wait on the LORD will find new strength." I'm sure that was just what the *waiting* exiles did not want to hear! I know it's not what I want to hear. Waiting wastes time. I don't even like red lights.

Isaiah knew that, so he proceeded to describe, in beautiful, divinely inspired words, the rewards of waiting. The divine promise for those who wait upon the Lord is a powerful incentive. I want renewed strength; I want to mount up with wings like eagles; I want to walk and not faint.

You might be wondering, *But how can waiting give me strength?* Albert Barnes's insights are helpful here:

> The word rendered "wait upon" here denotes properly *to wait*, in the sense of *expecting*. The phrase, "to wait on Jehovah," means to wait for his help; that is, to trust in him, to put our hope or confidence in him . . . It does not *imply* inactivity, or want of personal exertion; it implies merely that our hope of aid and salvation is in him.[2]

To wait means "to tarry, to look ahead confidently, to expect patiently." The one who waits does not rush ahead in her own strength. She trusts God to guide her.

The wisdom of depending on God's guidance was vividly depicted during Israel's wilderness experience. They were helpless without God's power for survival and His guidance for leading them out of the desert. His presence with them was manifested by a cloud in the daytime and a fire at night. The physical signs showed the way. Whenever the cloud lifted, the people marched. When it settled, they pitched their tents and waited until it lifted again. While the cloud remained in one place they went about their daily routines, but they were always in the process of waiting for God to continue guiding them.

This principle of waiting is applicable to us. Sheep should always wait for their shepherd to guide them. Whatever situation we are in, we do best to wait for the Lord to lead. Our prayer should be, "Lord, You know my circumstances. I do not want to rely on my own insight, so I will wait confidently for You to reveal to me the way I should go. I know that when I have no will of my own, I can more easily discern Your will through Your Spirit, through Your Word, and through open and closed doors. I will wait patiently for the cloud to lift before I make a decision, for I want Your presence to go with me."

Those who wait upon the Lord will discover that their weakness is changed to strength. They will be fully armored in the Lord, ready to do His will, because they have already submitted to His will by waiting and trusting.

Waiting means allowing God to use your life *as* He pleases, *when* He pleases. Anytime you allow God to be the Lord of your life, you will mount up on His wings, drawing nearer to Him. You will be able to say with David, "He fills my life with good things. My youth is renewed like the eagle's!" (Ps. 103:5 NLT). When you do not depend upon your own resources, but trust in and appropriate God's strength, you will run and not grow weary; you will walk and not become tired. No matter how deep the river you must cross or how intense the fire you must walk through, you will not faint. His grace will be sufficient. "Don't you know that the LORD is the everlasting God, the Creator of all the earth? He never grows faint or weary" (Isa. 40:28 NLT).

> Notice how, first, the prophet points to the unwearied God; and then his eyes drop from heaven to the clouded, saddened earth, where there are the faint and the weak, and the strong becoming faint, and the youths fading and becoming weak with age. Then he binds together these two opposites—the unwearied God and the fainting man—in the grand thought that he is the *giving* God, who bestows all his power on the weary. And see how, finally, he rises to the blessed conception of the wearied man becoming like the unwearied God.
>
> —R. Maclaren[3]

For Reflection

In what ways can "waiting on the Lord," as Isaiah described in 40:29–31, bring you closer to God?

Talk to the Lord about an area of your life in which you especially need to learn how to wait on Him.

KEY THOUGHT FOR DEEPER INTIMACY: *Waiting increases my dependence on the Father, drawing me into deeper trust and intimacy with Him.*

The Father speaks *(what is He saying to you?)*:

The child responds *(what are you saying to Him?)*:

PART FOUR

The Father's Joyful Embrace

THE FATHER AND THE CHILD

The child spoke:
> *Father, thank You for the security and strength You give me when I take hold of Your hand.*

My child, you are learning that you will draw your strength from quietness and trust.

> *Yes, I am beginning to understand that You are truly my Father who desires to guard and guide me.*

You are My child. I love you. I care about everything in your life. I want the best for you.

> *Father, the way is often perplexing and painful.*

It is so for all who live in the world. But I am your Father who redeems and who works all things together for good.

> *Sometimes it's difficult to see the good.*

All that matters for eternity is good.

> *Then I want to live for the eternal. I desire to live for You and Your purpose for me. I long to receive Your love and to experience Your arms holding me securely.*

It is My joy to reveal Myself to you, and it is My joy to embrace you.

22

I Will Be
Your Confidant

The secret [of the sweet, satisfying companionship] of the Lord have they who fear—revere and worship—Him, and He will show them His covenant, and reveal to them its [deep, inner] meaning.

—*Psalm 25:14 AMPLIFIED*

I recall the excitement I felt as a young girl when a friend cupped her hand over my ear and whispered something confidential. We would giggle as I was sworn to secrecy. From that time on, our shared secret united us in a special bond. As inconsequential as our little-girl secrets were, they nevertheless held an exclusiveness that was appealing. The secrets you were privy to depended on whose friend you were currently, so there was status attached to being let in on such confidences.

When the exclusiveness positioned me on the outside instead of the inside, I remember hearing the singsong refrain, "We've got a secret! We've got a secret!" It was sung by the insiders to taunt the one who had not been told the highly important information.

Gossipy secrets can separate, but as David testified in Psalm 25:14, precious truths shared between a Father and His child can nurture a growing intimacy.

THE SECRET OF FRIENDSHIP WITH GOD

The word *secret* can also be translated "friendship," as Derek Kidner explains: "*Friendship* is the Hebrew word sôd, meaning both 'council' and 'counsel': both the circle of one's close associates and the matters that are discussed with them."[1] David wrote knowingly about the special fellowship he shared with his Shepherd. Because he was the Lord's "close associate," he continually cried out to the Lord and sought the counsel of his Friend. In the Psalms we are privileged to have his wonderful record of the matters discussed between them, making us "insiders" to the confidences they shared.

David made it clear that this promise of intimacy is granted only to those who fear the Lord. The awe and reverence are prompted by love, not anxiety regarding future punishment. Fearing God means acknowledging His power and authority, not because we bow in grudging submission, but because we want to please Him in everything we do. It entails seeking Him first, trusting Him unconditionally, and loving Him with all the heart, mind, soul, and strength. The reward of such reverence is intimate knowledge of God Himself, as seventeenth-century writer Michael Jermin observed: "It is an honour to him to whom a secret is committed by another, a greater honour to him to whom the king shall commit his own secret; but how is he honoured to whom God committeth his secret? For where the secret of God is, there is his heart and there is himself."[2]

When we "revere" the Lord, we continually surrender our lives to Him in worship and obedience. In this profound respect we may come boldly to the throne of grace where we find mercy, help, and intimate companionship. David confidently wrote, "You can be sure of this: the LORD has set apart the godly for himself" (Ps. 4:3 NLT).

God draws close to those who draw close to Him, for He delights in our desire to revere His name and bring Him glory. He longs to share His heart with His children. One expression of this is the Lord's counsel, as David affirmed in this psalm: "Who are those who fear the LORD? He will show them the path they should choose" (Ps. 25:12 NLT). Only those who truly fear the Lord want Him to choose their path.

Friendship with God is reserved for those who fear the Lord. Within this special bond, God shares the secrets of His covenant. In this context *covenant* means "commands" or "law." God promises to give understanding of His purposes and intentions in what He has bound Himself to do for His people.

During the days of Noah, people had given themselves up to evil, and wickedness was rampant. God's solution was a great flood to destroy all the corruption and violence. But there was one righteous man living at that time, who feared the Lord and desired to do His will. The Scriptures tell us that Noah walked with God and enjoyed a close relationship with Him. Because he found favor with the Lord, Noah received God's grace and was informed of His secret plan: "I have decided to destroy all living creatures, for the earth is filled with violence because of them" (Gen. 6:13 NLT).

God also confided in Abraham, whom He chose to become the father of the nation of Israel. Abraham's faith drew him into such a close walk with God that he was known as God's friend. The Lord so highly regarded Abraham that when He was on His way to destroy Sodom and Gomorrah, He asked, "Should I hide my plan from Abraham?" (Gen. 18:17 NLT). Because Abraham feared and worshiped the Lord, he was made aware of God's purposes and intentions concerning the cities.

Daniel was another such close associate of the Lord. The godly young man of Judah was taken captive by King Nebuchadnezzar and lived the rest of his life in Babylon, becoming one of the king's wise men. One night Nebuchadnezzar had a disturbing dream. He called his magicians and astrologers to interpret his nightmare, and he wanted an explanation even though he refused to disclose what he had dreamed! The penalty for failure to provide an explanation was death to all wise men. The sentence included Daniel, who quickly asked for more time so that he and his friends could pray for God to give them the interpretation. And God answered: "That night the secret was revealed to Daniel in a vision" (Dan. 2:19 NLT).

The secret was not all that Daniel was privileged to hear from God, for he was also granted incredible visions of the future. Daniel's righteousness made him an intimate friend of God. His devotion was so unswerving that it cost him a night in the lions' den. He is an outstanding example of one who revered and worshiped God, and consequently enjoyed the sweet, secret, satisfying companionship of the Lord.

The apostle Paul was a zealous persecutor of the early church before he encountered the Lord Jesus on the road to Damascus. After Paul came to faith in Christ and was commissioned as a minister of the gospel to the Gentiles, he exchanged persecuting the Lord for experiencing intimate fellowship with Him. God entrusted Paul with the secret of His new covenant of grace. To reveal to Paul the deep, inner meaning of His purposes in the gospel, the Lord caught him up to paradise. Paul recorded in 2 Corinthians 12:2–4 that what he saw and heard was so astounding, he could not express it.

CHARACTERISTICS OF A CONFIDANT

These profound truths can be revealed only to those who fear and worship God. When Paul wrote to the Corinthians, he explained that the natural man cannot understand the truths of God because he does not have the Holy Spirit's instruction:

> But we know these things because God has revealed them to us by his Spirit, and his Spirit searches out everything and shows us even God's deep secrets . . . But people who aren't Christians can't understand these truths from God's Spirit. It all sounds foolish to them because only those who have the Spirit can understand what the Spirit means. (1 Cor. 2:10, 14 NLT)

I desire the sweet, satisfying companionship of the Lord, but it is a little intimidating to study the lives of Noah, Abraham, Daniel, and Paul. They were great men of God, chosen and set apart to serve Him. No wonder they received the deep meanings of God's ways! Yet the notable characteristic of each man is that *he walked with God.* That way of life is available to us as well.

Friends who walk together share secrets. This *walking* is also called *abiding.* Abiding allows the Holy Spirit to speak to your heart through His Word and prayer. It makes us available to the Lord to receive insight, revelation, and intimacy.

David indicated that the primary condition for intimacy is fear of the Lord. I revere the Lord by giving Him His rightful place in my life, by acknowledging my lowliness, weakness, and sinfulness in light of His greatness, power, and holiness. I obey Him by giving up the right to myself and humbly bowing down at His feet, fearing to displease Him and surrendering my will to His will. I fear the Lord by worshiping my Father, who loves me with an everlasting love.

If you, dear friend, truly desire for the Father to hold you close, do you show your deep respect for Him by your speech, by your choices, by your responses to people and circumstances? Do you have a dread of dishonoring His name? Do you pursue purity and holiness in your life? Do you walk with Him daily by reading His Word and praying to Him in secret? If your desire is to answer yes to these questions, then you will enter into the select council of God, where your heart will be filled to overflowing with insight into His heart.

It would seem that admission to the inner circle of deepening intimacy with God is the outcome of *deep desire.* Only those who count such intimacy a prize worth sacrificing anything else for, are likely to attain it. If other intimacies are more desirable to us, we will not gain entry to that circle . . . We are now, and we will be in the future, only as intimate with God as we really choose to be.

—J. Oswald Sanders[3]

For Reflection

How would you describe the blessings that result from fearing God, according to Psalm 25:14?

Spend some time in prayer, telling the Lord of your longing for His "sweet, satisfying companionship."

KEY THOUGHT FOR DEEPER INTIMACY: *The more I seek to fear God each day, the more I will experience His sweet companionship.*

The Father speaks *(what is He saying to you?)*:

The child responds *(what are you saying to Him?)*:

23

I Will Quiet
Your Soul

Lord, my heart is not haughty, nor my eyes lofty; neither do I
exercise myself in matters too great or in things too wonderful
for me. Surely I have calmed and quieted my soul, like a weaned
child with his mother; like a weaned child is my soul within me
[ceased from fretting]. O Israel, hope in the Lord from this time
forth and for ever.

—*Psalm 131:1–3* AMPLIFIED

A young man was being ridiculed for voicing his ideas. *He is but
a youth! How can he speak about such matters? What experience has he
had in public affairs? Such presumption—what ambition he must
have! Never have we witnessed such pride and conceit.* These words
pierced the soul of this modest, sensitive youth. He left the gather-
ing deeply wounded and went immediately to his favorite place to
meditate, examine his heart, and speak to his God. Picking up his
instrument, he began to sing, "Lord, my heart is not haughty . . ."

No one knows what circumstances prompted David's heartfelt
appeal, but the humility and devotion in this psalm exemplify his
entire life. From his early years, David was never considered some-
body special. When the prophet Samuel was commissioned to
anoint a new king of Israel after Saul was rejected for disobedience,
God told him to look among Jesse's sons. Samuel went out to meet

with Jesse, who brought out seven sons for the prophet's appraisal. Not one of them was the chosen one. Puzzled, Samuel asked Jesse if he had any other sons. Almost as an afterthought, Jesse told him, yes, but it was just the youngest one, who was out tending sheep. Samuel had to request that the boy be brought to him, and God revealed that he was the one. David had not even merited consideration by his own father. *O Lord, my heart is not haughty.*

While David was still a young shepherd, but after Samuel had anointed him the next king in front of his family, Jesse sent David on an errand to deliver food to his older brothers. They were fighting in Saul's army against the Philistines. David was speaking to his brothers when the giant, Goliath, taunted the Israelite army. Incensed, David said to the men nearby, "What shall be done for the man who kills this Philistine and takes away the reproach from Israel? For who is this uncircumcised Philistine, that he should defy the armies of the living God?" David's oldest brother, Eliab, angrily rebuked him: "Why did you come down here? And with whom have you left those few sheep in the wilderness? I know your pride and the insolence of your heart, for you have come down to see the battle" (1 Sam. 17:26, 28 NKJV). *O Lord, my heart is not haughty.*

For the next ten years, David endured Saul's persecution while waiting on God to remove Saul and his designated heir, Ishbosheth, from the throne. David never pushed himself forward. When Absalom, his own son, rebelled and took over his throne in Jerusalem, David left voluntarily. As he departed, he endured the cursing of Saul's relative, Shimei, without retaliating. *O Lord, my heart is not haughty.*

Whatever situation prompted David to write this lovely psalm, he was sincere in proclaiming to the Lord that his heart was not proud. He knew he was speaking to One who "searches all hearts and understands all the intent of the thoughts," as he told his son Solomon (1 Chron. 28:9 NKJV). David could hide nothing from the Lord. There was no false modesty in his prayer, just a childlike desire for comfort.

PRIDEFUL OR PEACEFUL

To be haughty is to be blatantly and disdainfully proud. The Pharisees provide an excellent role model of a vain and conceited heart. Remember the Pharisee who went to the temple to pray? He essentially thanked God that he was better than other men: "I thank you, God, that I am not a sinner like everyone else, especially like that tax collector over there!" (Luke 18:11 NLT). John wrote in his epistle that the boastful pride of life was not from the Father, but from the world (1 John 2:16). David, a man after God's heart, did not want to follow the world's way of haughtiness.

"Lofty eyes" concerned David too. They characterize someone who is contemptuous, scornful, and insolent. Have you ever studied faces? They often reveal a lot about the inner person. Scornful people don't have to say a word to reveal their attitude; their eyes sufficiently communicate their condescension. The writer of Proverbs stated that first on the list of the six things the Lord hates is "a proud look" (6:17 NKJV). In contrast, consider the tax collector who went to pray at the same time as the Pharisee. He was so humble that he could not even lift his eyes toward heaven. Instead, he beat his breast and prayed, "O God, be merciful to me, for I am a sinner" (Luke 18:13 NLT).

David continued to pour out his heart to God by declaring that he was not interested in great matters or in things too marvelous or profound for him. For David, such great matters could well have been ambitious, self-seeking pursuits. But he was not interested in advancing his own cause or seizing the throne. He was content to serve wherever God wanted him—guarding sheep, escaping from Saul, governing a nation. He did not seek the approval of other people by parading his knowledge or status.

David prayed for wisdom, but he was not going to allow himself to become anxious about difficult matters. He was secure enough in God that he didn't have to know everything. It wasn't that David didn't want to go deeper in his knowledge of God, for he asked the Lord to teach him:

Show me Your ways, O LORD;

Teach me Your paths.

Lead me in Your truth and teach me. (Ps. 25:4–5 NKJV)

David's humility kept him seeking God, not his own advancement.

In the eleventh century, Anselm prayed similar thoughts: "I do not seek, O Lord, to penetrate thy depths. I by no means think my intellect equal to them; but I long to understand in some degree thy truth, which my heart believes and loves. For I do not seek to understand that I may believe; but I believe, that I may understand."[1]

David's prayer indicates that the opposite of prideful ambition is a calm and quiet spirit. He was not driven to seek a position in life. The only position he wanted was that of a weaned child resting against his mother. His desire was to be content in the Lord, weaned from all the world had to offer: riches, honor, earthly pleasures.

A PICTURE OF TRUST

David had learned not to fret over what most people think is indispensable. In his spirit of submission, he was free from self. He illustrated that by describing a child who, after nursing, can sit peacefully in his mother's lap without anxiously demanding nourishment. Even though the mother is the one who has withdrawn what the child used to crave, the child still desires, and is comforted by, the mother's closeness. David used it as a picture of the soul at rest. Such childlike trust is a necessary quality for the kingdom of God.

One example of how David had been weaned from human cravings was his decision to spare Saul's life. The present king was in murderous pursuit of the future king, and he unknowingly entered the very cave where David and his men were hiding. David's men were amazed at the perfect opportunity for David to kill the one who was trying to kill him. Had he done so, he would have been safe, and the kingdom could have been his. But instead of murdering Saul, David cut off part of Saul's robe. That was the action of a man who had quieted his soul.

But even the act of cutting Saul's robe gave David an attack of conscience because he had dared raise his hand against the Lord's anointed. He would have been justified in slaying Saul, but he had been weaned from ambition and was waiting submissively for God to act in his life. David's deference was not the response of a man with a haughty heart.

David has much to teach us about the importance of restful trust in drawing close to God. His experience with the Lord led him to exhort all of Israel to hope in—to count on, have faith in, rest assured in, feel confident in—the Lord. Because he had calmed his soul, he no longer placed his hope in other people or in himself. It was a joy for him to let the Lord direct his life. He had placed his hope in God, and it was so freeing that he wanted everyone to hope as he did—forever.

I love how David could so confidently tell the Lord that his heart was not proud. I hate pride, especially in myself. I can so easily promote myself and display any little knowledge I have. But I don't want my life consumed with trying to get recognition or applause. Knowing that God is opposed to the proud is enough for me to ask Him to keep me from a haughty heart or lofty eyes. All I want is to be a contented child, resting in His arms, my sole ambition to be in His presence and in His will. What is the Lord's response to such a child? You may be sure it is His joyful embrace.

> Weaning takes the child out of a temporary condition into a state in which he will continue for the rest of his life: to rise above the world is to enter upon a heavenly existence which can never end. When we cease to hanker for the world we begin hoping in the Lord. O Lord, as a parent weans a child, so do thou wean me, and then shall I fix all my hope on thee alone.
>
> —Charles Spurgeon[2]

For Reflection

Why do you think David connected the absence of pride with quieting the soul in Psalm 131?

Following David's example, quiet your soul before the Lord with a prayer of trust.

KEY THOUGHT FOR DEEPER INTIMACY: *The opposite of pride is trust, and quieting my soul in trust will always bring me closer to God.*

The Father speaks *(what is He saying to you?)*:

The child responds *(what are you saying to Him?)*:

24

I Will Give You Rest

Come to Me, all you who labor and are heavy laden, and I will
give you rest. Take My yoke upon you and learn from Me, for I
am gentle and lowly in heart, and you will find rest for your
souls. For My yoke is easy and My burden is light.

—*Matthew 11:28–30* NKJV

Come and stay anytime you want to rest!" This comforting, enticing invitation has been extended to me by a dear friend who owns
a lovely A-frame getaway cabin on Mount Lemmon in Tucson. The
forty-five-minute drive is a relatively easy, though circuitous, climb
up to a refreshingly cool nine thousand feet. Once there, I am surrounded by pungent pine trees, aged mountain oaks, and lots of
quiet. I take a deep breath in my spirit, and everything that has
been demanding my immediate attention seems more willing to
wait now that I am on the mountain.

When I go to the cabin, my life is simplified. I rest and I work,
but the work is always done at the right pace. The questions always
arise, Why do I allow myself to become so harried and tired? Why
can't I live like this all the time?

The Lord Jesus came to save those who are heavily burdened.
He ate with tax collectors and sinners. He ministered to people
who were blind, had leprosy, were disabled, were possessed. He

cared for those who were oppressed by the religious system of the day. His heart continually went out to the "rest-less" multitudes, whom He fed spiritually as well as physically. To all of them, and to us as well, He issues a compelling, gracious invitation. The way to become unburdened is to accept His magnanimous call. The way to enjoy true rest is to come to Him.

AN INVITATION FROM OUR LORD

Come. Sometimes the hardest part of going to my friend's mountain cabin is making all the preparations necessary to leave. The benefits are wonderful, but I won't experience them unless I actually make the trip. However, *going* involves effort—planning, packing, driving.

The cabin is open and available; it waits for me to come. But still I find it hard to leave home. Why? *I might get more done if I just stay where I am,* I think. There are so many responsibilities, and there is so much to do. *I just can't leave. If I go up the mountain, I'll be out of touch.* I can control things only if I stay here in the valley, even though I need rest. Even though I am tired. Even though I don't see any end to all that is entrusted to me. *No, I can't go.* As appealing as is the offer to rest, I will pay a price to leave. And I'm not sure that going to the cabin will change anything anyway.

This word *come* is crucial to Jesus' invitation. His rest is available to all, all the time. But the responsibility is ours to respond. Choosing to come to Him requires that we admit our weakness—that is, our inability to live life in our own strength.

When we are ready to accept His offer of learning from Him instead of depending on ourselves, we are choosing to come. This "coming" might signify our need for a Savior, or it might be a confession of sin, an admission that we realize, *I can't control my life,* or simply a cry for help because of weariness. The Lord knew that coming to Him would entail recognition that a life lived apart from Him was a life full of ultimate restlessness.

This invitation is specifically for the weary. The search for true rest is ended once and for all in coming to Christ. But to find it, one must first *come.*

To Me. When we come to Christ, we come to God—a living being, not a cause, an ideology, a group, or a code of rules or traditions. Christianity in all its facets is based solidly on our *relationship* with the triune God. It is only in knowing the Lord personally as Savior and Lord that we are able to be indwelt by the Holy Spirit, who teaches and strengthens us to be obedient children of the Father.

Jesus was calling to all who heard Him to follow *Him,* not the religious traditions of the day. Life and rest are found in having a relationship with the living God, not in keeping a set of man-made rules.

All you who labor and are heavy laden. All who are striving in the world, all who are sinners, all who are discouraged, all who are hurt, all who are tired of self, all who are trying to please man, all who have no hope, all who are trying to earn their way to God, all who need a Savior—all are invited to come to Jesus.

Does life weigh heavily upon you? You always have a place to go for rest. Even better, you have a *Person* to go to.

And I will give you rest. This is not the vacation kind of rest we often seek. This is the rest and peace that only Christ can give: "rest from biting care; rest from bitter memory; rest from the chagrin of vain and wasted toil; rest from a reproaching conscience; rest from remorse."[1] It is rest given in the midst of doing what is right and pleasing to God. It is an inward rest that refreshes and renews us for continued service.

This rest produces a gentle and quiet spirit, giving the soul composure like that of a weaned child. This is the best rest of all, for it frees us from anxiety and worry, enables us to trust not in ourselves, but in the guidance and care of our Father.

Take My yoke upon you and learn from Me. To receive the rest Christ offers, you must take His yoke and learn from Him. The yoke pictured here is a double harness. If two people are in the same yoke, they are in agreement; they always go together; they experience constant fellowship. It is the perfect implement for tutoring—a young animal in training would be paired with an older, experienced animal to learn how to bear the yoke.

There is no doubt whose yoke this is—not ours, but Christ's. He wants to partner with us in order to teach us, guide us, and be with us. When we choose to be yoked with the Lord, we give up the right to our own ways in the commitment to become His disciples. We are in effect saying, *Lord, it is Your life now. David's prayer is mine as well:*

> Show me Your ways, O LORD;
> Teach me Your paths.
> Lead me in Your truth and teach me,
> For You are the God of my salvation;
> On You I wait all the day. (Ps. 25:4–5 NKJV)

When you commit to being eternally yoked with Jesus, you offer yourself as His disciple to serve as He pleases. You give up *your* life in order to receive the beauty, richness, graciousness, and peace of *His* life.

For I am gentle and lowly in heart, and you will find rest for your souls. How lovingly the Lord expresses His desire for us to come to Him. He assures us that He is not a harsh or condescending teacher, but humble and kind. Our Lord cannot teach without love, patience, kindness, goodness, and gentleness, for they form His inherent and unchanging character. We need not fear criticism or exasperation when we are taught by the Lord. The reality is that His teaching gives rest.

For My yoke is easy and My burden is light. To varying degrees, all of us carry burdens and are in some way yoked to someone or something else. The Lord offers an alternative to carrying our own burdens and being yoked to those people or things that take us in directions that increase our restlessness. In a sweeping and incomparable paradox, Jesus declared that His yoke was not like other yokes—His fits well and rests lightly. It does not chafe or need constant adjustment.

When compared with all other yokes, Christ's is easy. When compared with all other teachings, His is simple. His teaching can be obeyed in His strength. First John 5:3 (NKJV) confirms this truth: "His commandments are not burdensome."

This is an extraordinary invitation. It is written by the finger of God, at the cost of Jesus' sacrifice on the cross. His call echoes through the ages to all who will answer. He will not force you to come, but He does call you, and He waits for your response. What else could He do to make this invitation more appealing? Anytime you may come. He offers rest for your weary soul. He is gentle and humble. His yoke is easy and His teaching light. He waits where He longs to give cool refreshment: the highway is clear, the invitation printed in His Word. The decision to go to Him is yours.

He can give rest to the weary; he can refresh the toiling, anxious soul; he can give peace to the mind distracted by bewildering doubts. None could dare say this but only God. Put the words into the mouth of St. Paul or St. John, or any the very greatest of saints; for them to say such things would be arrogant, presumptuous in the extremest degree. But from the lips of the Lord Jesus Christ those great words were only the simple truth, words of tenderness and lowliness. The very fact that he stood there in human form, that he uttered those words in human language, that he had submitted to contradiction and rejection, proved his lowliness, his condescension. It would be far otherwise were he not, what we know that he was, the Almighty God.

—B. C. Caffin[2]

For Reflection

In what ways does Jesus' image of a yoke (Matt. 11:28–30) communicate rest and relief from burdens?

Study the steps Jesus lists in this passage that are necessary to experience the rest He is offering, and then spend some time with the Lord in prayer about them.

KEY THOUGHT FOR DEEPER INTIMACY: *The Lord's rest is always available to me, but I experience the benefits only when I choose to stay yoked with Him.*

The Father speaks *(what is He saying to you?)*:

The child responds *(what are you saying to Him?)*:

25

I Will Reward You with Joy

The kingdom of heaven is like a man traveling to a far country,
who called his own servants and delivered his goods to them.
And to one he gave five talents, to another two, and to another
one, to each according to his own ability; and immediately he
went on a journey.

—Matthew 25:14–15 NKJV

*O*nce upon a time there was a kind, wealthy king who was going on
a long journey. Before he left, he gave gifts of service to his attendants.

To one, the monarch entrusted the care of his entire castle.
Although the king would be gone, many of his extended family
members would be visiting during his absence, so this servant was
responsible to see that the castle remained ready for use.

To another servant, the king entrusted the vast expanse of his
personal gardens. This responsibility included tending the land,
maintaining the crops, and harvesting food for all who came.

A third attendant was asked to be responsible for the guest book.
He was to ensure that everyone signed the book when he visited, so
the king would have a record of who had enjoyed his hospitality
during his absence.

When the king left, he did not tell his servants when he would
return. Neither did he promise any rewards for their service. The

castle was his, the land was his, and the guest book was his. It was understood that the servants were expected to exercise good stewardship.

When the king returned to his estate, he called his attendants into his presence and asked them to give an account of how they had used their gifts of service.

The attendant in charge of the castle was eager to tell his master that the castle had received so many visitors that he had built several additional wings to accommodate everyone. The king was delighted with the servant's initiative and productivity in his name, and he enthusiastically rewarded the man.

The servant responsible for the gardens had expanded them to include a lovely flower garden for the guests to enjoy. Again the king was pleased with the creativity and industriousness of his servant in improving his kingdom. He gladly compensated the man.

The third attendant stood before the king, holding the guest book. It was still in its original condition; it had never been used. He immediately began defending his decision not to make the book available. People were always arriving at odd times, he said, so it was difficult to get everyone to sign. He didn't think the book should be used by some visitors and not others. He hadn't been all that sure the king *really* cared about having everyone's names recorded anyway. So he decided to hide the book in his room, and he was returning it to the king unused. The king was angry at his servant's laziness. For his utter lack of desire to please his master, he was terminated from the king's service.

By now you have recognized this as my paraphrase of Jesus' parable of the master who gave talents to his servants. Retelling it this way has helped me to think through the parable in order to understand the significance of the servants' varying gifts, how they responded to their master's assignments, and the judgments they received from him.

Jesus told this parable to help people understand the nature of faithful service in the kingdom of God. This teaching immediately followed His parable of the wise and foolish virgins, which illustrated the importance of watching, waiting, and preparing for the Lord's return. These two parables complement each other, for our lives are to combine serving and waiting. Both will lead us into deeper intimacy with the Father.

GIFTS OF SERVICE

Jesus taught His disciples that the kingdom of heaven is just like the kingdom of the king who entrusts his servants with gifts for promoting the welfare of his kingdom while he is away. All of the endowments are the king's, and he proportions them to his servants as he chooses.

Paul's explanation of the gifts of the Spirit echoed Jesus' parable: "But one and the same Spirit works all these things, distributing to each one individually as He wills" (1 Cor. 12:11 NKJV). One servant cannot legitimately compare or complain about the gift he was given because it is the Lord's sovereign choice.

Marcus Dods commented on this parable, "Each gets what each can conveniently and effectively handle, and no one is expected to produce results out of proportion to his ability and his means."[1]

I remember years ago when a number of my friends were planning their weddings and choosing their bridal parties. Sometimes I was asked to be a bridesmaid; other times I was asked to stand by the guest book. I always felt I had a lesser role as the guest book "guard," but that was the bride's choice. Had I declined to accept this responsibility because I felt it wasn't an important enough position, I would have been an unfaithful friend.

Although the gifts may differ, the same fidelity is required. However, God grants us free will in how we exercise our gifts. In the parable, when the king departed, the servants were left alone to do as they pleased. Servants are provided for, but unlike slaves, they are not forced to serve. The king trusted his servants to employ their gifts honestly and unselfishly because they loved their master. There was no thought of rewards; the only consideration would be to please and honor the one who gave the gift. When I have carefully chosen a gift for a friend, I am always pleased to see her wearing or using it.

We are not to hide our gift away simply because we might think it's too small and inconsequential to make a difference. Even though I thought that standing by the guest book was not as significant as being a bridesmaid, I learned that having this position enabled me to greet everyone and make all feel welcome. I think this is the attitude that the servant in my paraphrased story should have had. But he felt that the king had been unfair because all he had been given to look after was a guest book. Anyone could do that. Apparently, he was not very important to the king, or he would have been given a much more responsible job. He decided that his king was unfair and unjust, so he felt justified in doing nothing for him.

In Jesus' parable, the unworthy servant was called *wicked* and *lazy.* He was condemned because he did not exercise his gift at all. His was the smallest talent with the least responsibility, so his neglect is all the more inexcusable. Clearly, the results of the service are not at issue, but the faithfulness and willingness of the servant.

One day Jesus sat opposite the treasury and observed how people put in their money. He saw the rich give out of their abundance, and He saw a destitute widow give out of her poverty. Her *mites,* which she offered in sincerity of heart, were worth more to the Lord than all the coins given by the wealthy. She illustrated what Paul would later teach about giving: "For if there is first a willing mind, it is accepted according to what one has, and not according to what he does not have" (2 Cor. 8:12 NKJV).

In the Scriptures, the king told his lazy servant that even though he had only one talent, he could have given it to the bankers so at least some interest could have accrued. But the servant was not willing to do anything for the king, and for that he was judged.

THE REWARDS OF USING OUR GIFTS

Those who misjudge God, as the unworthy servant did, are never liberal toward Him. In fact, the servant slandered and accused the king. He said that the *king's* character and actions caused him to do nothing: "Lord, I knew you to be a hard man" (Matt. 25:24 NKJV).

How easy it is to rationalize that God is to blame for our sin. Matthew Henry observed,

> How could he know him to be so? . . . Does not all the world know the contrary, that he is so far from being a hard master, that *the earth is full of his goodness,* so far from reaping where he sowed not, that he sows a great deal where he reaps nothing? For he *causes the sun to shine, and his rain to fall, upon the evil and unthankful, and fills their hearts with food and gladness* who say to the Almighty, *Depart from us.* This suggestion bespeaks the common reproach which wicked people cast upon God, as if all the blame of their sin and ruin lay at his door, for denying them his grace. But if we perish, it is owing to ourselves.[2]

The grace extended to this servant lay dormant in his heart. He did not stir up the gift of God; he quenched the Spirit. He was not humble and repentant, but defensive and sullen.

In contrast to the wicked and lazy servant, the loyal servants were called *good and faithful.* What magnificent words for any servant to hear from his master: "Well done, good and faithful servant; you were faithful over a few things, I will make you ruler over many things. Enter into the joy of your lord." Although there seemed to be no equity in the gifts given, there was equity in the rewards. Both faithful servants, though they had differing talents, were made rulers over many things (Matt. 25:21, 23 NKJV). Isn't this incredible? God is not hard! He is more than fair. He is extravagantly gracious in His rewards.

All God asks is that you be His trusting, faithful servant, willing to serve wherever you are placed and equipped with the perfect gift to help build His kingdom. He doesn't want you to look at others to compare your gift with theirs or seek their approval. You are to look only to the King, desiring to serve Him wholeheartedly and faithfully. His praise and His joyful embrace are worth any sacrifice, even if you are only assigned to stand by the guest book in your Father's castle.

God's method is to take account of character, of motive, of the way in which a person makes use of what is entrusted to him. Thus they who produce most results will not be honoured more than those people whose efforts result in less visible effects, but who are equally faithful with their smaller gifts . . . Any good in the work we have done is only accomplished by means of the grace of God, and therefore we must say, "Not unto us, but unto thy Name be the glory." Yes, the glory is all God's. Still there is room for effort and fidelity. God acknowledges these qualities, and when he sees them he rejoices over them. In his great judgment he will generously acknowledge them.

—W. F. Adeney[3]

For Reflection

Read Jesus' parable in Matthew 25:14–30. What do you think the man who entrusted the talents to his servants hoped to accomplish by this act?

Communicate to the Lord your view of Him as a Master and your desire to be a worthy servant.

KEY THOUGHT FOR DEEPER INTIMACY: *I experience the Father's joyful embrace when I accept the gifts He has entrusted to me and serve Him faithfully wherever He has placed me.*

The Father speaks *(what is He saying to you?)*:

The child responds *(what are you saying to Him?)*:

26

I Will Set You Free from the World

God forbid that I should boast except in the cross of our Lord
Jesus Christ, by whom the world has been crucified to me, and
I to the world.

—*Galatians 6:14 NKJV*

The duplex was sixty-five years old. It was a plain white house
that sat two or three feet off the ground. A white wooden lattice
was wrapped around the bottom of the house to cover the pipes
underneath. There was a square cement front porch with two front
doors that had tattered black screens. The dwelling would never
receive a historic plaque. It was very ordinary—to be honest, it was
ugly—but it was the best place for us to live for a while.

My husband, Jack, had just bought a veterinary practice. This
"house," situated next door, came with the purchase. We had two
little ones, and I was six months pregnant with a third, so we needed
to use both sides of the duplex. The house was dark and cold with
cracked wallpaper. Although I had the use of two kitchens, neither
of them was very efficient. Since we were next door to the animal
hospital, we also had visiting rats in our walls. It was all pretty
depressing!

As we began to meet people and were invited to their rat-free,
attractively wallpapered homes, I was confronted with the idea of

entertaining friends in our veterinary "parsonage." *I can't have people in this house,* I thought. *Everyone else has a nice home—this one is a total embarrassment. I don't even have a dining room!*

Over the weeks as I wrestled with my pride, the Lord gently spoke to my heart: *Cynthia, until you are content with this home, I cannot trust you with another.* Thus began my understanding of what it means to be crucified to the world and to boast only in the Cross.

THE FREEDOM OF THE CROSS

Paul wrote the inspired words in Galatians 6:14 in the context of defending Christian liberty. Judaizers were teaching the necessity of circumcision in addition to faith. The legalists were trying to make Christianity into a sect of Judaism. In so doing, they could avoid persecution from the Jews by becoming circumcised, and from Rome by becoming officially sanctioned Jews.

Paul denounced the false teachers for not keeping the whole law, and he accused them of boasting about their converts to circumcision. Can't you just hear them? "Guess who just got circumcised? *I'm* the one who convinced him to do it!"

In great contrast to the Judaizers' boast of winning people to their works-oriented way to salvation, the apostle Paul wanted only to boast about the Cross. For it is the Cross, not circumcision, that saves. It is God's grace, not human effort, that brings about a new birth. Paul looked to the Cross alone for his glory.

In all its physical cruelty and spiritual splendor, the Cross represented the ultimate sacrifice for humanity's redemption. There is salvation by no other name but Jesus, and salvation by no other way but the Cross. It was an affront to Paul that anyone would proclaim another way, so he centered all his energies solely on the Cross. He wrote to the Corinthians, "I determined not to know anything among you except Jesus Christ and Him crucified" (1 Cor. 2:2 NKJV).

For the reformed Pharisee, the Cross was not only his salvation, but also freedom and joy in his relationship with God. Gone was the burden of the law. Gone was the rigid, legalistic way of life. Gone was the endless striving to perform. Through the Cross, the Lord Jesus had made him a new creation. Paul would never go back to his old life in which he could boast of being a Hebrew of Hebrews, a zealous Pharisee who was blameless in keeping the law. For Paul had experienced the glorious salvation of the Lord Jesus, creating a new life filled with liberty, love, and grace.

The Cross had reconciled and pardoned Paul, enabling him to say, "I have been crucified with Christ; it is no longer I who live, but Christ lives in me" (Gal. 2:20 NKJV). What a joy to trade his old life for Christ's life! How dare anyone boast in anything other than the costly, extravagant, life-giving cross of Christ.

The false teachers were concerned about what the world thought of their religious practices. They wanted to be accepted by the Jews as well as by the Romans, and they were willing to compromise the Cross. The world was ready to condemn and persecute those embracing only the Cross. The Cross plus circumcision would ensure the approval—and therefore the advantages—of the world. In contrast, Paul fervently declared that his interest in the world had died. The eternal joy of the Cross was much more attractive than the world or its opinions.

The Cross had crucified the world to Paul, and Paul to the world. It had so profoundly pierced his heart and changed his life that the world no longer captivated him. He knew he was in but not of the world. That was exactly where he wanted to be.

On His last night, Jesus counseled the disciples, "When the world hates you, remember it hated me before it hated you. The world would love you if you belonged to it, but you don't. I chose you to come out of the world, and so it hates you" (John 15:18–19 NLT). As the Lord's disciple, transformed by the Cross, Paul no longer belonged to the world. He was a pilgrim traveling through to a heavenly kingdom, and he had the scars from the world to prove that he was Christ's.

To the Philippians, Paul wrote of how the Cross radically changed his view of what was important. He recounted all his reasons for placing his confidence in being religious—he was circumcised, born into the tribe of Benjamin, a Pharisee, a zealous persecutor of the church, a strict adherent to the law. "I once thought all these things were so very important," he observed, "but now I consider them worthless because of what Christ has done. Yes, everything else is worthless when compared with the priceless gain of knowing Christ Jesus my Lord" (Phil. 3:7–8 NLT).

The trappings of the world—family heritage, leadership roles, social position, professional accomplishments—are ultimately worth nothing when compared with the blessing and acceptance found in the cross of Christ. Yet still we are tempted to cling to them because at first glance they look so gratifying. That was why the apostle John so strongly urged us to turn away from the lures of the world:

> Stop loving this evil world and all that it offers you, for when you love the world, you show that you do not have the love of the Father in you. For the world offers only the lust for physical pleasure, the lust for everything we see, and pride in our possessions. These are not from the Father. They are from this evil world. And this world is fading away, along with everything it craves. But if you do the will of God, you will live forever. (1 John 2:15–17 NLT)

As Paul concluded his letter to the Philippians, he thanked them for a gift they sent:

> Not that I was ever in need, for I have learned how to get along happily whether I have much or little. I know how to live on almost nothing or with everything. I have learned the secret of living in every situation, whether it is with a full stomach or empty, with plenty or little. For I can do everything with the help of Christ who gives me the strength I need. (Phil. 4:11–13 NLT)

Paul's interest in the world's allurements and comforts was dead. He was no ascetic, for he could live in abundance, but material possessions were no longer important. He could live in plenty, or he could live with little. Whatever his circumstances, he could rest content because of the Cross.

This was the lesson I was to learn in our family's early years: to be content, to boast only in the Cross. Could I be satisfied living in an old duplex? Could I live with little instead of much? Had the gospel transformed me to the point that wherever I was, I could get along happily because of the amazing love and grace God had lavished upon me from the cross? I knew God was asking me if that was enough—or did I need the world's finery and the approval of others to make me feel complete? Had I been crucified to the world? Was the Cross all that mattered to me?

My training period in that old house lasted four years. After three frustrating years of trying to plan for building our own home, we finally purchased a fairly new one. It was exquisite, and it had only one front door. It was made of brick, and it sat on the ground. The rooms were large and the kitchen was perfect, with an adjoining dining room. And there were no rats!

I knew I could learn to live quite contentedly in that home. But after just four years, the Lord led Jack to sell his practice and join a ministry organization. Could I leave the lovely home, knowing that I would never have another like it? Was I crucified to the world? Was the Cross my all?

Our street address in that home was Las Cruces, a Spanish word meaning "the crosses." I could not miss the message. Not only did I have to give up the new home, but in a sense, I had to continue to die to the world.

The incredible irony of the Cross is that out of death comes abundant life. When we understand that wonderful truth, there should be no question of dying to what the world offers and accepting what God gives. My experience with the old and new houses took place more than thirty years ago. How I praise God for teaching me the blessing of being content with where I am and what I have. It has made all the difference in my walk with God and my deepening intimacy with Him. I can say with Paul, "For my part, I am going to boast about nothing but the Cross of our Master, Jesus Christ. Because of that Cross, I have been crucified in relation to the world, set free from the stifling atmosphere of pleasing others and fitting into the little patterns that they dictate" (Gal. 6:14 *Message*).

> I take, O cross, thy shadow
> For my abiding place;
> I ask no other sunshine than
> The sunshine of His face,
> Content to let the world go by,
> To know no gain or loss,
> My sinful self my only shame,
> My glory all the cross.
>
> —Elizabeth C. Clephane[1]

For Reflection

Consider Paul's declaration in Galatians 6:14. How does becoming "crucified" to the world draw you into greater intimacy with God?

Begin asking God to teach you what it means to be crucified to the world.

KEY THOUGHT FOR DEEPER INTIMACY: *When I stop clinging to the world, I am free to step into my Father's embrace.*

The Father speaks *(what is He saying to you?)*:

The child responds *(what are you saying to Him?)*:

27

I Will Abide with You

Who may worship in your sanctuary, LORD?
    Who may enter your presence on your holy hill?
Those who lead blameless lives
    and do what is right,
    speaking the truth from sincere hearts.

—*Psalm 15:1–2 NLT*

$\mathcal{N}$o shirt, no shoes, no service . . . Wipe your feet on the mat before you step inside." Whether in public places or private dwellings, we are used to various protocols for entering someone else's business or house. Restaurants and commercial office buildings typically post smoke-free signs. My husband has sometimes worn a loaner sport coat and tie when dining out. Most churches foster an attitude of reverence in dress and behavior for people attending services. In Japanese homes, everyone takes off his shoes before entering. We have an unwritten rule in our home that young children don't jump on the furniture!

Everywhere in our world, there are established practices designed to maintain order and harmony among families, organizations, and communities. Just as we have created guidelines, so God has set forth what we might call laws of hospitality for dwelling in His sanctuary. These are not designed to keep people out, but to help us overcome obstacles of our own making to deeper intimacy with Him.

DWELLING IN THE HOUSE OF THE LORD

How can I dwell in the most intimate, abiding fellowship with the Lord? That was the question David asked in Psalm 15. It was in keeping with the wish he expressed in Psalm 27 to dwell with the Lord, and his affirmation in Psalm 23 that he would live in the house of the Lord all the days of his life. In Psalm 15, he inquired about the guidelines and standards for intimacy.

Some of us might read this psalm and assume that David was dividing the insiders from the outsiders. But David did not raise this question in seeking admission to God's home, for he was already God's child. Rather, he was asking about what was necessary to abide with the Lord. Who may *worship, sojourn, dwell* in Your sanctuary, tabernacle, or tent?

In David's time there were two tabernacles: the ancient one at Gibeon, and the new one where the ark was placed on Mount Moriah, known as the "holy hill." In the Old Testament, God dwelt in the tabernacle, or sanctuary. The particular dwelling was not at issue, for David's primary consideration was spiritual communion, living with God, desiring the Lord's divine presence and favor.

Who may live with You, Lord—Jehovah, the redeeming God of Israel? As David pondered this question, he was divinely inspired to write a profound response regarding godly personal character before God.

Certainly, our primary motivation for wanting to live with the Lord would be our great love for Him. Jesus referred to this love in His farewell discourse with the disciples: "All those who love me will do what I say. My Father will love them, and we will come to them and live with them" (John 14:23 NLT). If we love our Father, we will desire to please Him. We will want to reflect His character and obey His commands—to live in His sanctuary according to

His laws of hospitality. The reward for our desire to live in such a godly manner is close, intimate communion with our God.

WHAT IS A BLAMELESS LIFE?

Leading blameless lives is a characteristic of those who want to live in God's home. To be blameless is to be above reproach, to be virtuous and sincere. It is to walk with integrity—to practice honesty, trustworthiness, and faithfulness.

In the biblical sense, this does not mean to be perfect or sinless. The Scriptures are very clear that "all have sinned; all fall short of God's glorious standard. Yet now God in his gracious kindness declares us not guilty. He has done this through Christ Jesus, who has freed us by taking away our sins" (Rom. 3:23–24 NLT). We cannot be perfect, but we have been declared *not guilty* through Christ's sacrifice on the cross. We now have the Holy Spirit living within us, enabling us to lead lives, imperfect as they are, that can be blameless and pleasing to God.

Sincerity is the key to walking blamelessly. It means wholeheartedly and earnestly desiring to walk with Him and honor Him by the way we live. We *want* to obey; we *want* to be above reproach. The Lord looks at our hearts and sees our motives, and sincerity is an integral quality of those who dwell in God's sanctuary.

Uriah, the husband of Bathsheba, is a sterling example of one who walked uprightly. After David's sinful encounter with Bathsheba resulted in her pregnancy, David recalled Uriah from the siege of Rabbah. He was trying to cover up his sin by sending Uriah home to Bathsheba so that everyone would assume Bathsheba's pregnancy was by her husband.

When Uriah appeared before the king, David said to him, "Go on home and relax" (2 Sam. 11:8 NLT). But Uriah didn't go home.

"What's the matter with you?" David exclaimed. "Why didn't you go home last night after being away for so long?" (2 Sam. 11:10 NLT).

Uriah's reply revealed his sincerity and integrity: "The Ark and the armies of Israel and Judah are living in tents, and Joab and his officers are camping in the open fields. How could I go home to wine and dine and sleep with my wife? I swear that I will never be guilty of acting like that" (2 Sam. 11:11 NLT). Uriah had full permission from his king to be with his wife, but his desire to lead an upright life kept him from compromising his integrity. Uriah could worship in the sanctuary.

Paul is another example of one whose blameless life enabled him to enter the Lord's presence on His holy hill. This is evident in his words to the Corinthians: "We can say with confidence and a clear conscience that we have been honest and sincere in all our dealings. We have depended on God's grace, not on our own earthly wisdom. That is how we have acted toward everyone, and especially toward you" (2 Cor. 1:12 NLT).

TO DO WHAT IS RIGHT

To do what is right is another guideline for abiding in intimacy. Those who seek to live with God will want to do works of righteousness—acts that demonstrate holiness, goodness, and honor. We want to do what is right in relation to God and others. Paul wrote to the Ephesians, "You must display a new nature because you are a new person, created in God's likeness—righteous, holy, and true" (Eph. 4:24 NLT). God is our Father, and we should grow in Christlikeness. Our new nature should prompt us to do what is right.

I shop frequently at a large discount store. It is always crowded, and the checkout lines are usually long and slow. One day, after finding everything on my list, I headed to the checkout counters, dreading a lengthy wait. I was surprised to find a short line; I couldn't believe I was able to check out so quickly. It was a first!

As I was loading the bags into the car, I noticed a roll of paper towels in the bottom of the shopping cart that had not been paid for. I looked hard at that roll of towels; it was less than a dollar. The last thing I wanted to do was to go back into the store and wait in line. I was sure that one short line was all I was allotted in a lifetime. But I picked up the roll, walked into the store, stood in a long line, and paid for the towels. Why? Because I want to abide with my Father.

SPEAKING THE TRUTH FROM THE HEART

To worship in the Lord's sanctuary and enter into His presence, we must speak the truth from a sincere heart. Our words should spring from a pure and genuine spirit—this means not saying one thing while we mean another. That is what hypocrites do.

David pleaded with the Lord,

> Help, O LORD, for the godly are fast disappearing!
>   The faithful have vanished from the earth!
> Neighbors lie to each other,
>   speaking with flattering lips and insincere hearts. (Ps. 12:1–2 NLT)

Flattery and insincerity are barriers to worship.

Jesus emphasized the importance of this principle to the woman at the well: "God is Spirit, so those who worship him must worship in spirit and in truth" (John 4:24 NLT). David wrote of the vital relationship between truth and intimacy: "The LORD is near to all who call upon Him, to all who call upon Him in truth" (Ps. 145:18 NKJV).

When Nathan confronted David with his sin involving Uriah and Bathsheba, David didn't try to justify himself. He didn't try to manipulate the truth, and he didn't blame anyone else. David spoke the truth humbly and sincerely from his heart: "I have sinned against the LORD" (2 Sam. 12:13 NLT). He knew that those who speak truth in their hearts experience the presence of God.

The prodigal son, who took his inheritance and squandered it in sinful living, spoke truth from his heart when he said, "I will go home to my father and say, 'Father, I have sinned against both heaven and you, and I am no longer worthy of being called your son. Please take me on as a hired man'" (Luke 15:18–19 NLT). When the son returned to his father, he was welcomed, embraced, and given a celebration. In speaking the truth and recognizing his sin, he entered into the presence of his father.

If your desire is to dwell with your Father, you will naturally want to practice holiness. Because you love your Father and want to be intimate with Him, your journey will be one of integrity and honesty toward God and man. Your life will exemplify Matthew 5:16 (NLT): "Let your good deeds shine out for all to see, so that everyone will praise your heavenly Father." Your blameless walk and your determination to do what is right are for your Father's glory and your closeness to Him.

Speaking the truth in your heart will ensure that you acknowledge the truth about any sin or hypocrisy in your life. Abiding in Christ, who is the truth, assures you of having the truth in your heart. As a result, your speech will be sincere and honest toward God and others. Your Father does not expect your life to be perfect, but He does want you to be sincere and wholehearted in your desire to dwell with Him.

Lord, I would trust Thee completely; I would be altogether Thine; I would exalt Thee above all. I desire that I may feel no sense of possessing anything outside of Thee. I want constantly to be aware of Thy overshadowing presence and to hear Thy speaking voice. I long to live in restful sincerity of heart. I want to live so fully in the Spirit that all my thoughts may be as sweet incense ascending to Thee and every act of my life may be an act of worship.

—A. W. Tozer[1]

For Reflection

How do you think sinful people can follow the standards David set in Psalm 15:1–2 for dwelling with the Lord?

Pray that God will deepen within you the discernment necessary to live a blameless life.

KEY THOUGHT FOR DEEPER INTIMACY: *Living righteously means that I am free to enjoy my Father's abiding presence.*

The Father speaks *(what is He saying to you?)*:

The child responds *(what are you saying to Him?)*:

28

I Will Satisfy
Your Deepest Longings

O God, you are my God;
 I earnestly search for you.
My soul thirsts for you;
 my whole body longs for you
in this parched and weary land
 where there is no water.
I have seen you in your sanctuary
 and gazed upon your power and glory.
Your unfailing love is better to me than life itself;
 how I praise you!

—Psalm 63:1–3 NLT

All Israel has joined Absalom in a conspiracy against you!" (2 Sam. 15:13 NLT). How those words must have pierced David's heart! His own son was intent on seizing his throne.

David barely had time to think, but he knew that if he did not leave soon, Jerusalem might be destroyed. Hurriedly, David and his main household and troops evacuated the city. In deep sadness, the people watched them leave.

David and his group left Jerusalem by the road leading to Jericho, taking them through the northern part of the desert of Judah. David stopped at the shallows of the Jordan River. The

Scriptures paint this portrait of the exiled king: "David walked up the road that led to the Mount of Olives, weeping as he went. His head was covered and his feet were bare as a sign of mourning" (2 Sam. 15:30 NLT). As if the news wasn't bad enough already, David learned that his close friend and counselor, Ahithophel, had stayed in Jerusalem to advise Absalom. He was betrayed not only by his son, but by a good friend as well. Further disheartening him, Shimei, a distant relative of Saul, threw stones at him while yelling, "Get out of here, you murderer, you scoundrel!" (2 Sam. 16:7 NLT).

Weary and distressed, David and his people rested on the bank of the Jordan. Evening came on. David was in the wilderness spiritually as well as physically. He fell to his knees, lifted up his hands, and cried, "O God, you are my God" (Ps. 63:1 NLT).

David was addressing God as *Elohim*—"the Strong One, my strong God, my tower of strength."[1] In his sorrow, David called out with passion to his powerful Defender and Deliverer. He was not strong, but his God was. The Lord was his Shepherd, whom he knew intimately. The cry was a spontaneous and natural acknowledgment of God's love and sovereignty for a child in the wilderness. His prayer demonstrated the highest confidence in the One it addressed, and the deepest desire in its declaration of longing for God.

David searched "earnestly" for God. Some translations render this word *early*, which carries with it an allusion to the dawn.[2] Above and before all else, David sought the Lord. Circumstances did not hinder his search. In the midst of such turmoil and hurt, we might understand if David had chosen to indulge in self-pity. But he did not. His one thought was to pursue the sweet communion he knew he could experience only with the Lord.

A YEARNING OF BODY AND SOUL

David vividly expressed the intensity of his yearning through the image of thirsting in a land without water. His soul was thirsty; his very flesh longed for the living God. I live in the desert, where we are well acquainted with the need for water in a parched landscape. You can postpone hunger, but not thirst. When David described his soul as thirsty, he was communicating his critical need to drink from the living fountain.

John recorded another desert scene, involving a weary man and a desperate woman who met at the well of Jacob in the heat of mid-day. Naturally, they began discussing water. She was surprised that He, a Jew, would ask her, a Samaritan, to give Him a drink. He told her that if she knew who He was, *she* would be asking *Him* for a drink of "living" water. She questioned Him about this water. How would He get it? Where would it come from? And how could it be better than the water of their ancestor, Jacob?

In response to her questions, Jesus replied, "People soon become thirsty again after drinking this water. But the water I give them takes away thirst altogether. It becomes a perpetual spring within them, giving them eternal life" (John 4:13–14 NLT).

David's prayer in Psalm 63 pointed to this living water. David knew that only God can fully satisfy our deepest needs and longings.

The Hebrew word for "longing" occurs only in this passage, and it indicates an intense fervency. It literally means "pines" or "faints with desire."[3] David pined for the spiritual refreshment that accompanies God's presence. It is significant that he said his *body* longed to be renewed. Usually, the flesh wars against the spirit, but when the spirit's yearning reaches this pitch of intensity, the body responds accordingly. David's entire being affirmed that his only true need was to be in the presence of God.

The king had gazed upon the Lord's power and glory in the sanctuary, but he was in the wilderness, and he longed for the same glorious communion. Charles Spurgeon wrote,

> He longed not so much to see the sanctuary as to see his God;
> he looked through the veil of ceremonies to the invisible One . . .
> It is a precious thought that the divine power and glory are not

confined in their manifestation to any places or localities . . .
David did not thirst for water or any earthly thing, but only for
spiritual manifestations.[4]

PRAISE AMID DESPAIR

How many of us would be tempted to blame God for letting us
down if family and close friends turned against us? Having lost the
love of his son and of a special friend, David could yet praise God
for His unfailing love. Even though he had been forced to flee his
throne and was in the wilderness, his life filled with uncertainty,
David's perspective was centered on the eternal loving-kindness of
God. Difficult circumstances paled in comparison to his Father's
unconditional, everlasting love.

David could go so far as to proclaim that God's infinite love
meant more to him than life itself. Because David so deeply
longed for and believed in the Lord's presence, he could not help
singing praises to God. Praise recognizes the greatness of God
and springs from a heart overflowing with love and gratitude.
Though from the world's point of view David was destitute, he
knew that God had not forsaken him. He could not help praising God. Elsewhere David observed, "All who seek the LORD will
praise him. Their hearts will rejoice with everlasting joy" (Ps.
22:26 NLT).

C. S. Lewis described praise and worship as intimate giving—
of ourselves to God, but ultimately of God to us:

> I did not see that it is in the process of being worshipped that
> God communicates His presence to men. It is not of course the
> only way. But for many people at many times the "fair beauty of
> the Lord" is revealed chiefly or only while they worship Him
> together. Even in Judaism the essence of the sacrifice was not
> really that men gave bulls and goats to God, but that by their so
> doing God gave Himself to men; in the central act of our own

worship of course this is far clearer—there it is manifestly, even physically, God who gives and we who receive.[5]

With a broken heart, David sought God, offering no complaints—only praise. The praise brought him into the communion he craved. He concluded the psalm with vows to honor the Lord as long as he lived, to meditate in the night watches, to sing for joy in the shadow of His protecting wings, and to follow closely, for the Lord's strong right hand would hold him securely.

After a time of communion and prayer, David rose from his knees confident that those plotting to destroy him would come to ruin. As for the king, he would rejoice in God.

DRAW NEAR TO GOD

If you are seeking intimacy with your Father, David's example of drawing near to God is priceless in its inspiring and practical help. When crushing circumstances surround you and you are forced into the wilderness, call to your Father as His child. Seek, thirst, and long for the Lord's presence above all. Let the Lord know that you want to behold His power and glory. Declare that His love is enough to see you through any wilderness. Praise His name, His goodness, His unfailing love, His mercy, His faithfulness.

And know that as you praise the Lord amid circumstances that break your heart, you will gain perspective, and you will experience His presence. Commit your way to Him, confident that He will hold you securely and that He will deal with injustice in His way and His time.

Henri J. M. Nouwen described a profound truth about intimacy with God:

> Now I wonder whether I have sufficiently realized that during all this time God has been trying to find me, to know me, and to love me. The question is not "How am I to know God?" but "How am I to let myself be known by God?" And finally, the

question is not "How am I to love God?" but "How am I to let myself be loved by God?" God is looking into the distance for me, trying to find me, and longing to bring me home.[6]

The Father's longing to hold you close is far stronger than your desire for Him to hold you. His love for you is everlasting. He desires to teach you and guide you as His own child. He is honored when you seek Him first with your whole being. He delights in hearing your voice and in delivering you through your trials for your good. He promises to be with you and strengthen you when you experience times of temptation, when you walk through deep waters, and when you grow weary beyond enduring. The Lord invites you to come to Him humbly to receive rest and reward. He wants you to be free from the world's demands and to be worthy of dwelling in His sanctuary. Your Father wishes to bring you close to His heart, and He waits expectantly for you to draw near to Him, thirsting for His presence.

The Lord's overall purpose is that you know Him intimately as your Father who unceasingly longs to hold you close.

It is no wonder that the Psalm was adopted by the early Church as its morning Psalm . . . "The Fathers of the Church," says St. Chrysostom, "appointed it to be said every morning, as a spiritual song and a medicine to blot out our sins; to kindle in us a desire of God; to raise our souls, and inflame them with a mighty fire of devotion; to make us overflow with goodness and love, and send us with such preparation to approach and appear before God."

—A. F. Kirkpatrick[7]

For Reflection

What kinds of experiences would bring someone to declare, as David did in Psalm 63:1–3, that the Lord's love is better than life itself?

Using David's prayer in this psalm, spend some time with the Lord expressing your desire to know Him more intimately.

KEY THOUGHT FOR DEEPER INTIMACY: *Truly thirsting for my Father's presence places me inside His loving embrace.*

The Father speaks *(what is He saying to you?):*

The child responds *(what are you saying to Him?):*

THE FATHER AND THE CHILD

The Father spoke:
My child, we have had some special times together.

Yes, we have. I am overwhelmed with Your desire to be my Father.

I am pleased that you realize how much I love you.

What can I do so that I will not forget Your love and care?

Can we keep meeting in secret? Can you love My Word and continue to listen for My voice?

I think I can. I want to spend the rest of my life deepening my intimacy with You.

If that is your desire, then nothing can separate us.

Thank You for being a Father who whispers words of love, who listens, who is always with me to strengthen and guide me.

I will continue to be your God, who has set His love upon you.

And I will continue to be Your child, who thirsts and longs for Your presence.

Then be assured, My precious child, that I will always hold you close.

Notes

Chapter 1: You Are Mine!

1. Robert Jamieson, A. R. Fausset, and David Brown, *Commentary on the Whole Bible*, rev. ed. (Grand Rapids: Zondervan, 1961), 563.
2. Michael Phillips, *A God to Call Father* (Wheaton, Ill.: Tyndale, 1994), 48.

Chapter 2: My Love for You Is Everlasting

1. Matthew Henry, *Commentary on the Whole Bible* (Iowa Falls: Riverside, n.d.), 4:594.
2. W. F. Adeney, in *The Pulpit Commentary*, ed. H. D. M. Spence and Joseph S. Exell (Peabody, Mass.: Hendrickson Publishers, n.d.), 11:16–17.

Chapter 3: I Am the One Who Leads You

1. Henry, *Commentary*, 4:272.
2. Oswald Chambers, *My Utmost for His Highest* (Westwood, N.J.: Barbour & Co., 1935), Jan. 30.

Chapter 4: You Have the Right to Be My Child

1. Jane Austen, *Pride and Prejudice* (New York: Penguin, 1985), 365–66.
2. H. R. Reynolds, in *The Pulpit Commentary*, 17:14.
3. Henry, *Commentary*, 5:852.
4. *The New King James Study Bible* (Nashville: Thomas Nelson, 1977), note on Matthew 1:21.
5. Lewis Sperry Chafer, *He That Is Spiritual* (Grand Rapids: Zondervan, 1967), 32.

Chapter 5: Seek First My Kingdom

1. B. C. Caffin, in *The Pulpit Commentary*, 15:246.

Chapter 6: I Dwell with the Humble

1. G. Rawlinson, in *The Pulpit Commentary*, 10:107.
2. T. Delitzsch, in *The Pulpit Commentary*, 10:360.
3. Albert Barnes, *Barnes' Notes* (Grand Rapids: Baker, 1998), 1:323.

4. Frederick W. Faber, quoted in *Joy and Strength*, ed. Mary Wilder Tileston (Minneapolis: World Wide, 1988), Aug. 31.

Chapter 7: I Will Deliver You

1. *The New King James Study Bible*, note on Psalm 91:14.
2. Paraphrased from Barnes, *Barnes' Notes*, 3:15–16.
3. Mary B. M. Duncan, in *The Treasury of David* by Charles Spurgeon (McLean, Va.: MacDonald, n.d.), 2:111.
4. James Strong, *Concise Dictionary of the Words in the Hebrew Bible*, in *The Hebrew-Greek Study Bible*, ed. Spiros Zodhiates (Iowa Falls: Word Bible Publisher, 1988), 40.
5. Phillips, *A God to Call Father*, 90–91.

Chapter 8: He Hears My Voice

1. Wilson Mizner, *Quotable Quotations*, comp. Lloyd Cory (Wheaton, Ill.: Victor Books, 1985), 219.
2. Brother Lawrence, quoted in *Closer Than a Brother*, by David Winter (Wheaton, Ill.: Harold Shaw, 1971), 37–38.

Chapter 9: He Answers Me

1. R. Tuck, in *The Pulpit Commentary*, 3:310.
2. Ibid., 3:311.

Chapter 10: He Invites Me to Be Alone with Him

1. John Chrysostom, quoted in *Pathway to the Heart of God*, by Terry W. Glaspey (Eugene, Oreg.: Harvest House, 1998), 132.
2. François Fenelon, quoted in *Pathway to the Heart of God*, 53.

Chapter 11: He Gives Me Words to Pray

1. J. Oswald Sanders, *Prayer Power Unlimited* (Minneapolis: World Wide, 1977), 42, 97.
2. Lawrence O. Richards, *Expository Dictionary of Bible Words* (Grand Rapids: Zondervan, 1985), 194.
3. Andrew Murray, *With Christ in the School of Prayer* (Old Tappan, N.J.: Revell, 1953), 31.

Chapter 12: He Teaches Me How to Spend My Days

1. Oswald Chambers, in *The Oswald Chambers Daily Devotional Bible* (Nashville: Thomas Nelson, 1992), reading 37.
2. William Seeker, in *The Treasury of David*, 11:81.

Chapter 13: He Cleanses My Heart

1. Condor and Clarkson, in *The Pulpit Commentary*, 8:131.

2. Ezekiel Hopkins, in *The Treasury of David*, 1:292.

Chapter 14: He Draws Me to His Heart

1. W. Forsyth, in *The Pulpit Commentary*, 8:205.
2. "From a Broad Sheet in the British Museum," quoted in *The Treasury of David*, 1:12.
3. A. W. Tozer, *The Pursuit of God* (Camp Hill, Pa.: Christian Publications, 1982), 97.

Chapter 15: He Is with Me in Life's Deep Waters

1. *Foxe's Book of Martyrs*, ed. W. Grinton Berry (Grand Rapids: Baker, 1978), 26.
2. Amy Carmichael, *Gold by Moonlight* (Fort Washington, Pa.: Christian Literature Crusade, n.d.), 55.

Chapter 16: He Strengthens Me to Resist Sin

1. William Gurnall, *The Christian in Complete Armour*, rev. and abr. (Carlisle, Pa.: Banner of Truth, 1986), 1:84–85.
2. Ibid., 1:49–50.

Chapter 17: He Prepares Me for Life's Struggles

1. T. Croskery, in *The Pulpit Commentary*, 20:268–69.
2. Barnes, *Barnes' Notes*, 132.
3. Gurnall, *The Christian in Complete Armour*, 1:65, 67.

Chapter 18: He Guides Me Through Life

1. Derek Kidner, *Psalms 1–72* (Downers Grove, Ill.: InterVarsity, 1973), 121.
2. F. B. Meyer, *The Life of Paul* (Lynnwood, Wash.: Emerald Books, 1995), 105.

Chapter 19: He Takes Care of Me

1. Phillip Keller, *A Shepherd Looks at Psalm 23* (Grand Rapids: Zondervan, 1970), 21.
2. Ibid., 35ff.
3. Spurgeon, *The Treasury of David*, 1:355.
4. Ibid., 1:354–55.
5. Amy Carmichael, *Whispers of His Power* (Old Tappan, N.J.: Revell, 1982), Sept. 8.

Chapter 20: He Never Leaves Me

1. Keller, *A Shepherd Looks at Psalm 23*, 61–62.
2. Spurgeon, *The Treasury of David*, 1:355.
3. Keller, *A Shepherd Looks at Psalm 23*, 83.
4. A. F. Kirkpatrick, *The Book of Psalms* (Grand Rapids: Baker, 1982), 127.
5. Barnes, *Barnes' Notes*, 211.
6. Keller, *A Shepherd Looks at Psalm 23*, 94–97, 99–100, 102.

7. Frances de Sales, quoted in *Streams in the Desert,* ed. Mrs. Charles E. Cowman (Grand Rapids: Zondervan/Daybreak, 1965), Feb. 8.

Chapter 21: He Strengthens Me When I Am Weary

1. W. Clarkson, in *The Pulpit Commentary,* 2:88.
2. Barnes, *Barnes' Notes,* 76–77.
3. R. Maclaren, in *The Pulpit Commentary,* 2:95.

Chapter 22: I Will Be Your Confidant

1. Kidner, *Psalms 1–72,* 116.
2. Michael Jermin, in *The Treasury of David,* 1:409.
3. J. Oswald Sanders, *Enjoying Intimacy with God* (Chicago: Moody, 1980), 20.

Chapter 23: I Will Quiet Your Soul

1. Quoted by N. McMichael in *The Treasury of David,* 3:140.
2. Spurgeon, *The Treasury of David,* 3:138.

Chapter 24: I Will Give You Rest

1. P. C. Barker, in *The Pulpit Commentary,* 15:466.
2. B. C. Caffin, in *The Pulpit Commentary,* 15:458–59.

Chapter 25: I Will Reward You with Joy

1. Marcus Dods, in *The Pulpit Commentary,* 15:500.
2. Henry, *Commentary,* 5:376.
3. Adeney, in *The Pulpit Commentary,* 15:496.

Chapter 26: I Will Set You Free from the World

1. Elizabeth C. Clephane, "Beneath the Cross of Jesus," in *Hymns for the Family of God* (Nashville: Paragon Associates, 1976), 253.

Chapter 27: I Will Abide with You

1. Tozer, *The Pursuit of God,* 127.

Chapter 28: I Will Satisfy Your Deepest Longings

1. G. Rawlinson, in *The Pulpit Commentary,* 8:22.
2. Kirkpatrick, *The Book of Psalms,* 353.
3. Ibid.
4. Spurgeon, *The Treasury of David,* 2:66.
5. C. S. Lewis, *Reflections on the Psalms* (San Diego: Harcourt Brace Jovanovich, 1958), 93.
6. Henri J. M. Nouwen, *The Return of the Prodigal Son* (New York: Doubleday/Image, 1994), 106.
7. Kirkpatrick, *The Book of Psalms,* 353.

About the Author

$\mathcal{C}$ynthia Heald is an author and speaker known to many women through her best-selling Bible studies and books, including *A Woman's Journey to the Heart of God.*

A native Texan, Heald graduated from the University of Texas with a B.A. in English. She and her husband, Jack, a veterinarian by profession, are on full-time staff with The Navigators. They have four grown children and six grandchildren and reside in Tucson, Arizona.

Also by Cynthia Heald

Becoming a Woman of Excellence (1986, NavPress)
Intimacy with God Through the Psalms (1987, NavPress)
Loving Your Husband (1989, NavPress)
Loving Your Wife, with Jack Heald (1989, NavPress)
Becoming a Woman of Freedom (1992, NavPress)
Becoming a Woman of Purpose (1994, NavPress)
Abiding in Christ: A Month of Devotionals (1995, NavPress)
Becoming a Woman of Prayer (1996, NavPress)
A Woman's Journey to the Heart of God (1997, Thomas Nelson)
A Journal for the Journey (1997, Thomas Nelson)
Becoming a Woman of Grace (1998, Thomas Nelson)